THE OFFICIAL SCRIPT BOOK
COMPLETE WITH ANNOTATIONS AND ILLUSTRATIONS

THE OFFICIAL SCRIPT BOOK
COMPLETE WITH ANNOTATIONS AND ILLUSTRATIONS

SCREENPLAY BY
DAVID KOEPP

BASED UPON THE NOVEL BY
MICHAEL CRICHTON

AND ON ADAPTATION BY
MICHAEL CRICHTON AND MALIA SCOTCH MARMO

ANNOTATIONS BY
JAMES MOTTRAM

INSIGHT
EDITIONS

Introduction

One of the most beloved movies of all time, Steven Spielberg's *Jurassic Park* (1993) owes its origins to the brilliance of author Michael Crichton. When Crichton began writing *Jurassic Park*, he was already firmly established as one of America's most successful novelists. Techno-thrillers like *The Andromeda Strain* (1969), which focused on the outbreak of an extraterrestrial microorganism, and *The Terminal Man* (1972), the story of a computer scientist who undertakes radical brain surgery, had established him as a fiction writer whose stories often took place at the cutting edge of science.

In 1974, he wrote the novel *Dragon Teeth*, a story about two rival paleontologists in the American West during the late nineteenth century, at a time when fossil hunting was at its most competitive. Although he would fail to find a publisher for *Dragon Teeth*

at the time, the world of paleontology remained an obsession. Gradually, he began brewing a more contemporary dinosaur-themed story, *Jurassic Park*.

The book would hit stores on November 20, 1990, but Crichton had been researching it for almost a decade. Recalled Crichton, "I remember in the early '80s, walking on the beach with Marvin Minsky, who is at the AI Lab at MIT, and saying in this very tentative way, 'I'm thinking about doing a story about a genetically engineered dinosaur' and waiting to see if he would make fun of me. And he said, 'Oh, well, yeah, that could probably be done one day' which I found very encouraging."[1]

---

1   "The Real Jurassic Park," *Nova*, Season 20, Episode 15, 1993

PAGE 2 Promotional art for the 30th anniversary of *Jurassic Park* captures the Main Road attack scene from inside a tour vehicle, as a fearful-looking Tim and Lex come face-to-face with the mighty *Tyrannosaurus rex*.

ABOVE An early *Jurassic Park* concept sketch by artist John Gurche depicts raptors in a sinister haunted house–like setting.

OPPOSITE An early *Jurassic Park* poster concept by Gurche, complete with the film's main characters reflected in a dinosaur's eyeball.

Initially, Crichton conceived the idea as a movie script, focusing on a young graduate student who secretly clones a pterodactyl from fossil DNA. Realizing that it would be almost impossible to keep such a science project under wraps, Crichton reworked the concept and decided to write it as a novel. Set on Isla Nublar, a fictional island off the coast of Costa Rica, the story centered on a billionaire visionary named John Hammond. Leasing the island from the Costa Rican government, Hammond is building a theme park like no other.

With the Environmental Protection Agency sniffing around, and his investors concerned, Hammond decides to bring in a group of experts for the weekend to road test his new attraction. Paleontologist Dr. Alan Grant, whose digs in Snakewater, Montana, have been funded by the Hammond Foundation, and his graduate student, paleobotanist Dr. Ellie Sattler, are among the guests. Also in attendance is chaos theorist Dr. Ian Malcolm and lawyer Donald Gennaro, whose company Cowan, Swain, and Ross are among the investors in the venture.

To their amazement, they witness a miracle: Jurassic Park is a habitat for living, breathing dinosaurs. Working through his bioengineering company InGen, Hammond's team, led by chief geneticist Dr. Henry Wu, have

been able to extract dinosaur blood from mosquitoes fossilized in amber for millions of years, extracting the DNA and using it to bring these creatures back to life.

Joining the tour party are Hammond's grandchildren, Tim and Lex, whose parents are going through a divorce, and the park's PR manager Ed Regis. As the tour gets underway, the group beholds a series of dinosaur wonders from a mighty *Tyrannosaurus rex* to a sick *Stegosaurus*. In the Control Room, overseeing the tour is John "Ray" Arnold, the chief engineer, and Robert Muldoon, the park's gamekeeper. Also present is Dennis Nedry, responsible for designing the sophisticated computer systems that keep the park running.

Nedry, however, has been compromised. Lewis Dodgson, from rival biotech firm Biosyn, has enticed him to steal embryos from Hammond's labs. With a storm approaching, Nedry is forced to make his move, switching off the park's security systems as he snatches the contraband. On the way to the dock, Nedry meets his demise after his jeep runs aground, and a frill-necked *Dilophosaurus* blinds him with its venom before ripping him open. Further chaos reigns as the electrified fences used to contain the dinosaurs lose their charge and the exhibits escape their paddocks.

ABOVE A conceptual painting by Tom Cranham, depicting Alan Grant and John Hammond's grandchildren looking toward the Jurassic Park Visitor Center.

OPPOSITE A concept sketch by John Gurche shows the *T. rex* in motion.

T-REX
vs Grant, Tim & Lex

① Guys round mountain heading for heli-pad.

10.7.91

2

... stops suddenly ...

3

PAN off Jeep
reveal mountain-slide wiped-out bridge...

Hammond's nature preserve soon becomes a feral, hostile environment. Shortly before the tour party enters the *T. rex* paddock, Lex spots escaped juvenile *Velociraptors*—agile, vicious predators that hunt in packs—sneak onto a supply ship heading for the mainland. Having escaped its paddock, the *T. rex* appears, tearing apart the Toyota Land Cruiser carrying Tim and Lex. Regis abandons the vehicle in terror, later to meet his maker when he is attacked by a juvenile *T. rex*. Malcolm is also badly injured, although Muldoon and Gennaro later find him and take him back to the park's secure compound, where Arnold and the others desperately try to regain control.

Separated from the others, Grant protects the children as he escorts them back through the park, a journey that includes further narrow misses with the *T. rex* along the park's river and at a waterfall, and a dangerous trip into a giant aviary. Meanwhile, the raptors hunt the survivors, trying to chew through the bars of the rooftop at the Safari Lodge where Malcolm and the others are now ensconced. While Arnold and Wu are both killed by the savage raptors, Grant is able to get the power back on when he returns to the compound with the kids.

In a hugely tense encounter, Tim and Lex manage to evade another raptor in the park's kitchen, with Tim locking the creature in a walk-in freezer. Meanwhile, Grant, in self-defense, poisons three more raptors, while Tim also resets the computer

Grant takes the wheel
— kids grab on!...

systems, allowing Gennaro to contact the supply ship carrying the stowaway raptors and command it to turn back from the mainland. While many of the surviving members of the tour group and staff are saved by the Costa Rican military, Malcolm succumbs to his injuries, and Hammond is eaten by a group of *Procompsognathus* aka "Compys"—knee-high scavenger dinosaurs with deadly razor-sharp teeth. The book ends with the island and its genetically resurrected wildlife being bombed by the military, as "white-hot explosions" engulf Hammond's paradise.

Such was the vivid nature of the book that when Crichton's agents began shipping the project around Hollywood, a bidding war ensued. The rights went to Steven Spielberg, the famed director of *E.T. the Extra-Terrestrial* (1982) and *Raiders of the Lost Ark* (1981), who would partner with Universal Pictures on the project. Crichton was originally brought onboard to adapt the book himself. After delivering his first draft on September 7, 1990, he then worked on a revised draft, dated January 19, 1991. At this point, he stepped away from the project. "Michael was happy to say, 'I've just taken my best shot. I'm kind of written out on the screenplay front. I have another book I want to write so you can do anything you want with it,'" says Spielberg.

Even before they had a final shooting script, Spielberg and producer Kathleen Kennedy assembled a cutting-edge team to bring the film's dinosaurs to life on the big screen. This group included Stan Winston, the special makeup effects expert who famously created the 14-foot Alien Queen animatronic for James Cameron's *Aliens* (1986). Joining him would be Michael Lantieri, responsible for the on-set special effects,

and pioneering stop-motion animator Phil Tippett, who had worked on George Lucas's original *Star Wars* trilogy (1977–1983). The brilliant visual effects supervisor Dennis Muren, from Lucas's visual effects house Industrial Light & Magic (ILM), was also hired.

This quartet, along with Spielberg, Kennedy, and production designer Rick Carter (who had just worked with Lantieri on *Back to the Future Part II*) regularly met to discuss how to bring scenes like the *T. rex* attack on the Land Cruiser to life. Storyboard artists, including Marty Kline, Dave Lowery, and Tom Cranham, were on hand to illustrate key scenes as ideas poured forth. While the dinosaur effects were still being worked on, Spielberg stepped away to direct the Peter Pan tale *Hook* in the early part of 1991.

THESE PAGES Early storyboards conceptualize an idea that never made it into any *Jurassic Park* script draft, as Grant, Tim, and Lex are chased by a *T. rex* as they head for the helipad in a jeep.

During this hiatus, Carter penned a script in the wake of Crichton's drafts. It was never meant as an official contribution to the scripting process, but rather as a way of assembling the myriad ideas that had been suggested during the development process. "I realized that the only way for me to see how the ideas might actually play out in the story was for me to 'collage' them into Michael's latest script," he explained, in a note dated March 7, 1991. He set out to create a working document, but "one thing led to another" and he began to shape it into a traditional screenplay.

Work continued on the dinosaur effects, with Spielberg planning to create the creatures using a blend of Tippett's stop-motion techniques and Winston's animatronic dinosaurs. Meanwhile, the search for another writer continued, as Spielberg and Kennedy began to cast their net wide. Playwright Tom Stoppard, with whom they'd worked on the 1987 J.G. Ballard adaptation *Empire of the Sun*, was considered. "I know that they had a deep connection at that point," recalls Carter. "And so I think that Kathy in particular, thought Tom could, in a sense, adapt himself to do almost anything."

Ultimately however, Kennedy turned to another candidate, Malia Scotch Marmo, who had just scripted *Hook*. The opportunity arose when Scotch Marmo's husband urged her to read *Jurassic Park* after hearing Amblin had bought the rights. "Kathy Kennedy saw me [reading the book] sitting on a golf cart on the lot outside of the *Hook* studio," recalls the writer. "She

asked what I thought so far." It wasn't long before she was hired to take a pass at adapting Crichton's work. Beginning work in October 1991, Scotch Marmo found Spielberg's guidance was invaluable during this time. "He made me see that each page must work on a number of levels at once," she says. "It should be weighty with narrative ingenuity."

Although Scotch Marmo's draft, which she completed on March 14, 1992, was impressive, Spielberg felt the script didn't quite land. To take it to the next stage, Spielberg decided to bring in David Koepp, who had co-written the 1992 fantasy *Death Becomes Her*, directed by Robert Zemeckis. Starting from scratch, the screenwriter impressed the director with his take on the novel, but in reality Crichton's book, filled with diagrams and charts, was a daunting adaptation. Says Koepp, "I remember lying on the sofa in my office, reading the book and thinking, 'That's gotta go, that's gotta go, that's gotta go. How the hell would I do that?' Over and over again."

Crichton's book wasn't his only road map to writing *Jurassic Park*. By now, due to the film's long development process, two years' worth of storyboards and script ideas were available to the writer. "Steven had these very large handfuls of gems, with set pieces and bits of philosophy and visual ideas and character ideas," says Koepp. "He had all this stuff. And he dropped it on a conference table and said, 'Put this together! Please! Quickly!'" Scenes like the *T. rex* Main Road attack and the raptor attack in the kitchen were locked in: "He had that. He just didn't know who the characters were." Scotch Marmo remained on hand to offer advice. "I was sending memos to Steven about David's draft," she recalls.

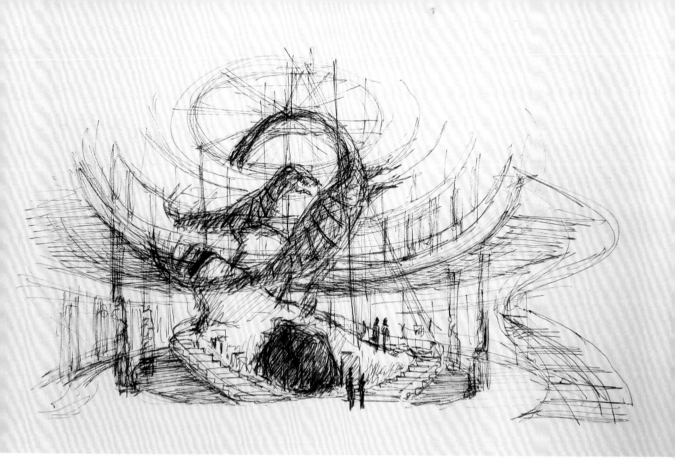

By this point, radical change was afoot. Explains Spielberg, "I had planned to do most of the movie with Stan Winston's full-scale animatronics. And I had earmarked about 65 [to] 70 shots that would be Phil Tippett's 'Go-Motion' animals." Tippett's "Go-Motion" was a variation on stop-motion animation that incorporated motion blur into each frame of animation, creating added realism. Over at ILM, however, a digital revolution was underway: Animators Steve "Spaz" Williams and Mark Dippé had used computer generated (CG) effects to animate a walking CG *T. rex* skeleton, while fellow animator Eric Armstrong created a running herd of *Gallimimus*. After running a number of tests, ILM eventually created versions of these creatures with realistic skin and muscles. "That completely convinced me that there was no going back," says Spielberg, who decided to abandon Go-Motion in favor of digital dinosaurs.

In tandem with these developments, Koepp delivered his first draft, dated April 23–May 1, 1992. It was now just three and a half months before

production on *Jurassic Park* was due to start in Hawaii, with the lush island paradise serving as the perfect embodiment of Isla Nublar. With cinematographer Dean Cundey in charge of shooting the picture, filming got underway on August 24, 1992. Key cast included Sam Neill as Dr. Alan Grant, Laura Dern as Dr. Ellie Sattler, Jeff Goldblum as Dr. Ian Malcolm, and Sir Richard Attenborough as John Hammond.

Koepp's revisions continued into the shoot, working with Spielberg every step of the way. "I had a collaborator who was absolutely gushing with ideas," says the writer. "It was more a case of me managing the firehose of good ideas that was directed at me." Even after the crew returned from Hawaii to complete the shoot back in Los Angeles, scenes were tweaked and improved as Spielberg visualized how to get the best out of Michael Crichton's novel. A movie phenomenon was about to be hatched, destined to revolutionize visual effects. Yet, behind it all, lay *Jurassic Park*'s deftly written screenplay, a template for one of modern cinema's most showstopping thrillers.

ABOVE An early sketch of the Visitor Center by production designer Rick Carter.

OPPOSITE PAGE A sketch by concept artist Mark "Crash" McCreery depicts a sleeping *T. rex*.

The Annotated Screenplay

PAGE 12 Promotional art
for the 30th anniversary
of *Jurassic Park* shows the
luckless Dennis Nedry cowering
as the deadly *Dilophosaurus*
extends its colorful frill.

ABOVE InGen workers stand
guard as the latest delivery
for Jurassic Park, a caged
raptor, arrives on Isla Nublar.

OPPOSITE BOTTOM Early
concept art by John Bell shows
a raptor in a child's bedroom,
an idea taken from Michael
Crichton's original novel.

EXT JUNGLE - NIGHT
An eyeball, big, yellowish,
distinctly inhuman, stares raptly
between wooden slats, part of a
large crate. The eye darts from side
to side, alert as hell.

A legend tries to place us - -

ISLA NUBLAR
120 MILES WEST OF COSTA RICA

- - but to us it's still the middle
of nowhere.

It's quiet for a second. A ROAR
rises up from the jungle,

deafening. The trees shake as
something very, very large plows
ahead through them, right at us.
Every head gathered in this little
clearing snaps, turning in the
direction of the sound as it bursts
through the trees.

It's a bulldozer. It drops its scoop
and pushes forward into
the back end of the crate, shoving
it across the jungle floor towards
an impressive fenced structure that
towers over an enclosed section of
thick jungle. There's a guard tower
at one end of this holding pen that
makes it look like San Quentin.

The bulldozer pushes forward into
the back end, the crate THUDS TO THE
FLOOR. A door slides open in the
pen, making a space as big as the
end of the crate.

Nobody moves for a second. A grim
faced guy who seems to be in charge
(ROBERT MULDOON, although we don't
know it yet).

                    MULDOON
        Alright now, pushers move in.
           Loading team move it.

The movement has agitated whatever is
inside the crate, and the whole thing
shivers as GROWLS and SNAPS come from
inside. Everyone moves back.

                MULDOON (cont'd)
       Alright, steady. Get back in there
     now, push. Get back in there. Don't
          let her know you're afraid!

The men go back to the crate and
begin to push it into the slot.

BEGINNINGS

The opening scene of the *Jurassic Park* screenplay went through multiple revisions. The prologue of Michael Crichton's novel begins with the aftermath of a *Velociraptor* attack, as Ed Regis and two workers escort a young colleague, lacerated by the claws of the deadly predator, to local medic Dr. Roberta Carter on the Costa Rican mainland. Crichton's first draft dispensed with this, instead leaping straight to a scene set on a Montana dig site that would introduce central protagonists Dr. Alan Grant and Dr. Ellie Sattler.

In his revised draft, Crichton opened with a variation on the novel's second major sequence, where a young vacationer, Tina, is attacked on a deserted Costa Rican beach by a Compy. He also includes another early scene from the novel, set at New York's Tropical Disease Lab, in which one Dr. Richard Stone and his technician Alice examine Tina's sketch of the Compy, with Stone reaching the conclusion it's a lizard.

Scotch Marmo's draft would revert back to the idea of swiftly introducing Grant and Sattler at a dig site during the film's opening moments, although her script begins with a close-up sequence focusing on a mosquito lodged within "an amber tomb," a needle extracting its blood. Conversely, the opening of Koepp's first draft dipped back into the novel, featuring Regis's trip to see Dr. Carter with the injured worker. Koepp was a big fan of the novel's intro: "It's a very strong opening. The rain-lashed hospital. And the guy brought in and they're trying to cover it up." Koepp also added a scene at the very beginning, not seen in the book, showing the raptor's claw slashing the poor worker.

When Koepp gave Spielberg the first half of the script, the director loved it but had an important note on the opening scene. Recalls Koepp, "He said, 'It's going great. But this opening . . . I feel like I've done that.' And I said, 'Oh, shit! It's *Jaws*.'" Indeed, when Regis tells the doctor the raptor attack was a "construction accident," a claim the physician casts doubt upon, the sequence of events recalled the scene in Spielberg's classic shark thriller, where Richard Dreyfuss's marine biologist examines the body of the first victim and famously says, "This is not a boat accident." For his final draft, Koepp dropped the hospital scene and instead wrote a sequence in which the audience witnesses the worker meeting his demise. "It works a lot better as an incident that we're watching unfold instead of something we're hearing about," he says.

RAPTOR PEN
GUARD

J. BELL 6·92

The crate THUDS UP AGAINST THE
OPENING. A green light on the side of
the pen lights up, showing contact
has been made.

FROM INSIDE THE CRATE,
we get glimpses of what's on the
other side of those wooden slats - -
jungle foliage, MEN with rifles,
searching searchlights. The view
is herky-jerky as the crate is put
into position.

                    MULDOON
Well locked Loading team, step away.
     Joffrey, raise the gate.

A WORKER climbs to the top of the
crate. The searchlights are trained
on the door.

The RIFLEMEN throw the bolts on
their rifles and CRACK their stun
guns, sending arcs of current
CRACKING through the air.

The Worker gets ready to grab the
gate when all at once - -

A ROAR comes from inside the crate,
and the panel flies out of his hands
and SMACKS into him, knocking him
clear off the crate.

Now everything happens at once. The
Worker THUDS to the jungle floor,
the crate jerks away from the mouth
of the holding pen, an alarm BUZZER
sounds - -

- - and a claw SLASHES out from
inside the crate. It sinks into the
ankle of the Worker, dragging him
toward the dark mouth between the
crate and the pen. The Worker SCREAMS
and paws the dirt, leaving long claw
marks as he is rapidly dragged toward
the crate.

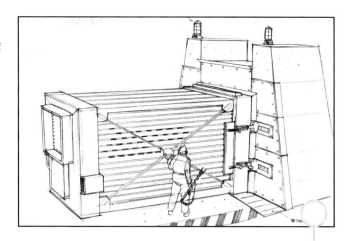

FATAL CLAW

Koepp's first draft sees the park worker edge toward the crate where an unseen *Velociraptor* is stashed, although at this stage it's not clear what's inside: "A claw flashes out from inside the crate, the worker SCREAMS . . ." As grisly as this is, Koepp's final version is far more chilling, with the raptor "leaving long claw marks" as the worker is "rapidly dragged toward the crate." This opening also introduces Muldoon, who did not feature in any earlier iteration of the scene. In this final draft, Muldoon refers to the worker as "Joffrey," a nod to the actor who plays him, Jophery C. Brown, a former baseball player for the Chicago Cubs who became one of the first Black stuntmen in America.

Muldoon SHOUTS orders:

                    MULDOON
   Tasers get in there, Goddamn it!

They FIRE their guns - the wood of
the crate SPLINTERS. Muldoon runs in
and grabs the Worker, trying to pull
him free.

The wild arcs of currents from the
stun gun flash and CRACK all around,
but in a second - -

- - the Worker is gone.

TOP A detailed sketch by
John Bell depicting the
raptor containment unit.

OPPOSITE Early concept art
by John Bell for raptor pen
guard uniforms, complete
with claw-motif symbol.

MINE CRAFT

Not featured in the novel, the Mano de Dios Amber Mine scene that appears in the final shooting script introduces one of Crichton's key ideas, as workers scour the Dominican Republic facility, looking for amber that contains fossilized mosquitoes filled with dinosaur blood. Koepp's first draft, however, differs from the final version. In that earlier iteration, John Hammond is present at the mine, with Gennaro telling him that the family of the savaged construction worker is filing a $2 million lawsuit. Hammond also reveals that they paid $22 million for the mine. He even speaks Spanish. "El perfecto! Exactamente lo que queremos! Perfecto!" he says, as he tosses a lump of amber to Gennaro. Dropping Hammond from the scene in his final draft, Koepp instead introduced the character of Juanito Rostagno (played by Miguel Sandoval in the film), who oversees the mining operation. The lawsuit has now swelled to $20 million, and it's here that Gennaro sets up the idea that an on-site inspection of Hammond's park is needed to reassure the investors and pacify the insurance company. The draft contains extra lines from Rostagno not seen in the finished film, notably at the very end of the scene, in which he holds up a lump of amber to the light and speaks to it in Spanish: "Oh you're so beautiful. You will make a lot of people happy."

CUT TO:

EXT MOUNTAINSIDE - DAY
MANO DE DIOS AMBER MINE
DOMINICAN REPUBLIC

DONALD GENNARO, forty, in a city man's idea of hiking clothes and a hundred dollar haircut, approaches on a raft being pulled across a river by TWO MEN.

On the hillside, JUAN ROSTAGNO, thirty-ish, Costa Rican, a smart-looking guy in workers clothes, is waiting for him.

ROSTAGNO
Tengo mil pesos que dicen que se cae.

(I have a thousand pesos that say he falls.) (or)

Apuesto mil pesos que se cae.

OPPOSITE TOP The "bloodsucking lawyer" Donald Gonnaro, played by Martin Ferrero.

RIGHT Conceptual art by John Bell shows the discovery of a lump of amber, with a mosquito encased inside it, at the Mano de Dios mine.

(I bet a thousand pesos he falls.)

Gennaro finally lands, and Rostagno helps him off the raft.

> GENNARO
> Hola, Juanito.

> ROSTAGNO
> Hola, bienvenido.

Rostagno leads Gennaro towards the mine. Dozens of shirtless WORKERS claw and SCRAPE at a rocky mountainside that is the site of an extensive mining operation. The work is all done by hand, pick and shovel instead of dynamite and bulldozer.

> GENNARO
> What's this I hear at the airport Hammond's not even here?

> ROSTAGNO
> He sends his apologies.

DONALD GENNARO

In Koepp's final draft, Donald Gennaro arrives at the mine "in a city man's idea of hiking clothes and a hundred-dollar haircut," although in the film itself he would wear a suit in this scene.

Crichton's novel gives more background on the character that did not make it to the final film. Gennaro came to Cowan, Swain, and Ross from a background in investment banking, and one of his earliest tasks was to help Hammond seek funding for InGen, eventually helping him raise almost a billion dollars. Gennaro's firm owns 5 percent of InGen, having invested in Hammond's wild schemes—in the book, Gennaro's boss, Daniel Ross, has grave doubts about Hammond and refers to him as "a potentially dangerous dreamer." The book also reveals that Gennaro is married, to Elizabeth, and has a four-year-old daughter Amanda, whose birthday falls on the very weekend that Gennaro must fly down to Costa Rica.

In Crichton's screenplay drafts, Gennaro introduces himself as "Don Gennaro, of Cowan, Swain, and Gennaro"—his boss Daniel Ross dropped from the narrative. Scotch Marmo, however, reinstates Ross in her draft, describing him as "a powerful black man who waves a prosthetic arm." His conversation with Gennaro echoes that of the novel, as they discuss Hammond and the company's 5 percent stake. "Don't be afraid to screw Hammond and burn Jurassic Park to the ground," Ross advises Gennaro, a dramatic expansion on the novel's dialogue where Ross simply tells him to "Screw Hammond."

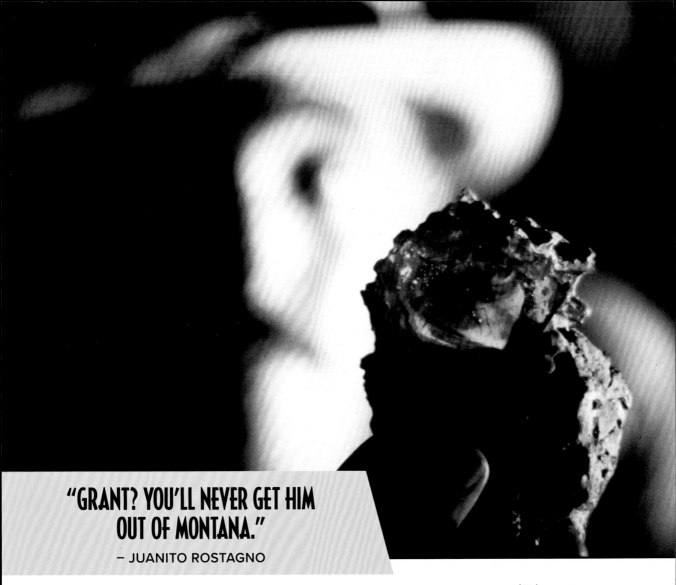

"GRANT? YOU'LL NEVER GET HIM OUT OF MONTANA."

– JUANITO ROSTAGNO

ABOVE Juanito Rostagno (Miguel Sandoval) holds up the latest amber find at the Mano de Dios mine.

GENNARO
You're telling me that we're facing a $20 million lawsuit from the family of that injured worker and Hammond couldn't even be bothered to see me?

ROSTAGNO
He had to leave early to be with his daughter. She's getting a divorce.

GENNARO
I understand that.

(or)

I'm sorry to hear that. We'd be well advised to deal with this situation now. The insurance company - -

Gennaro almost falls, Rostagno helps him.

GENNARO (cont'd)
- - the underwriters of the park feel the accident raises some very serious questions about the safety of the park, and they're making the

investors very anxious. I had to promise I would conduct a thorough on-site inspection.

                    ROSTAGNO
Hammond hates inspections. They slow everything down.

                    GENNARO
Juanito, if they pull the funding, that will really slow things down.

                     (or)

If they pull the funding that's going to slow things down around here.

A WORKER hurries up to them and busts into the conversation, breathless.

                    WORKER
                (to Rostagno)

Jefe, encontramos otro mosquito, en el mismo sitio.

(Chief, we found another mosquito in the same place.)

                    ROSTAGNO
            Seguro? Muestrame!

        (Are you sure? Show me.)

The Worker and Rostagno scramble back deeper into the mine. Rostagno calls back over his shoulder to Gennaro.

                ROSTAGNO (cont'd)
It seems like it's going to be a good day after all. They found another one! C'mon.

Gennaro struggles to keep up.

EXT CAVE - DAY
ROSTAGNO and GENNARO move into the dark, dripping cave, where at least a dozen other WORKERS are gathered in a tight circle, staring at something intently.

Rostagno fights his way to the center of the group. One of the WORKERS hands him something and Rostagno examines it carefully.

It's a chunk of amber, a shiny yellow rock about the size of a half dollar.

                    GENNARO
    If two experts sign off on the island, the insurance guys'll back off. I already got Dr. Ian Malcolm, but they think he's too trendy. They want Alan Grant.

                    ROSTAGNO
Grant? You'll never get him out of Montana.

                    GENNARO
                Why not?

                    ROSTAGNO
Because he's like me. He's a digger.

Rostagno turns and holds the amber up to the sunlight streaming through the mouth of the cave.

With the light pouring through it, the amber is translucent, and we can see something inside this strange stone - -

- - a huge mosquito, long dead, entombed there.

                    ROSTAGNO
                (smiles)

    Hay que lindo eres. Vas hacer a mucha gente feliz.

(Oh you're so beautiful. You will make a lot of people happy.)

DR. ALAN GRANT

In the novel's acknowledgements Crichton mentions drawing upon the work of "many eminent paleontologists" including John Horner. Better known as Jack, Horner was the chief template for Dr. Alan Grant. Described in the novel as a "barrel-chested, bearded man of forty," Grant's look in the novel closely matches Horner's appearance in real life. "I think [Jack's] enthusiasm for the dinosaurs informs the character," comments Sam Neill, the New Zealand–born actor who was cast as Grant. The book itself even casts them as contemporaries. As Crichton writes, in reference to the *Maiasaur*: "With John Horner, Grant had been the first to describe the species." In reality, even though Horner would serve as an advisor on *Jurassic Park*, he didn't meet Crichton until after the film was complete. "The first time I met him was in the limousine on our way to the premiere!" Horner says.

CUT TO:

EXT THE DIG - DAY

An artist's camel hair brush carefully sweeps away sand and rock to slowly reveal the dark curve of a fossil - it's a claw. A dentist's pick gently lifts it from the place it has laid for millions of years.

Pull up to reveal a group of DIGGERS working on a large skeleton. All we see are the tops of their hats. The paleontologist working on the claw lays it in his hand.

GRANT
(thoughtfully)

Four complete skeletons . . .

such a small area . . .

the same time horizon - -

ELLIE
They died together?

GRANT
The taphonomy sure looks
that way.

ELLIE
If they died together, they lived
together. Suggests some kind of
social order.

DR. ALAN GRANT, mid-thirties, a
ragged-looking guy with intense
concentration you wouldn't want
to get in the way of, carefully
examines a claw.

ABOVE An early Alan Grant
concept sketch by John Bell,
depicting the paleontologist
with beard and shorts.

OPPOSITE AND LEFT
New Zealand actor Sam
Neill was cast as Dr. Alan
Grant, a character inspired
to some degree by real-life
paleontologist Jack Horner.

"THEY HUNTED AS A TEAM. THE DISMEMBERED TENOTOSAURUS BONE OVER THERE - THAT'S LUNCH."
– ALAN GRANT

DR. ELLIE SATTLER, working with him, leans in close and studies it too. She paints the exposed bone with rubber cement. Ellie in her late twenties, athletic-looking. There's an impatience about Ellie, as if nothing in life happens quite fast enough for her.

Her face is almost pressed up against his, she's sitting so close.

ABOVE Dr. Ellie Sattler (Laura Dern) and Dr. Alan Grant (Sam Neill) at the dig site in Snakewater, Montana.

OPPOSITE LEFT An early sketch by John Bell that conceptualizes a potential look for Dr. Ellie Sattler.

OPPOSITE RIGHT Actress Laura Dern as Sattler.

GRANT (cont'd)
They hunted as a team. The dismembered tenontosaurus bone over there - that's lunch. But what killed our raptors in a lakebed, in a bunch like this? We better come up with something that makes sense.

ELLIE
A drought. The lake was shrinking - -

GRANT
(excited)

That's good. That's right! They died around a dried-up puddle! Without fighting each other. This is looking good.

From the bottom of the hill a voice SHOUTS to them:

VOLUNTEER (o.s.)
Dr. Grant! Dr. Sattler! We're ready to try again!

Grant SIGHS and sits up, stretching out his back.

GRANT
I hate computers.

DR. ELLIE SATTLER

Described in the book as "twenty-four and darkly tanned," with her blonde hair tied back, Dr. Ellie Sattler proved to be a difficult role to cast. "Steven sent me clips of young actresses to play Ellie," recalls Scotch Marmo. "The clips showcased the actresses in previous film roles. I noticed they were all ingénues. They had youth and a certain naïveté and freshness. I kept thinking they were missing the mark. Ellie is a scientist. Perhaps because my father was an astrophysicist, I couldn't buy the actors he was showing me as realistic in any way . . . in a science fiction movie like *Jurassic Park* believability was essential. Steven is very open to push back, and he asked, 'Who would you like?'" The writer made a case for Laura Dern, who coincidentally had impressed Spielberg in the 1985 film *Smooth Talk*. Adds Scotch Marmo, "Laura Dern had it all for me. She is an excellent actress so I thought she will draw out an honest portrayal of a scientist and she has the natural heft of intelligence and insight and personal power that would easily maintain her professional stature and earned status with the otherwise almost all male cast."

He shoves the claw absent-mindedly into his pocket and he and Ellie walk toward the source of the voice. As they walk, we get our first look at the badlands. Exposed outcroppings of crumbling limestone stretch for miles in every direction, not a tree or a bush in sight.

> # "WHAT ARE YOU DOING THERE!? EXCUSE ME! CAN YOU JUST BACK OFF? THIS IS VERY FRAGILE! ARE YOU OUT OF YOUR MIND?
>
> # GET OFF THAT AND GO FIND YOUR PARENTS!"
>
> – ALAN GRANT

THE KID

Then thirteen years old, Whit Hertford was cast as the boy—just called "KID" in Koepp's final draft—who gets spooked by Dr. Alan Grant during the Montana dig site sequence. Raised in Oak Park, California, Hertford had been acting for several years, beginning on the TV show *The Fall Guy*. He only spent two days on *Jurassic Park*, acting amid the 125-degree heat of the Mojave Desert. Although Hertford's time on set was brief, he shot an additional scene from Koepp's final draft that wouldn't make it to the final movie, where the boy kicks dirt onto one of the digs, and then mutters "asshole" as Grant scolds him.

In the dig itself, the ground is checkered with excavations everywhere. There's a base camp with five or six teepees, a flapping mess tent, a few cars, a flatbed truck with wrapped fossils loaded on it, and a mobile home. There are a dozen VOLUNTEERS of all ages at work in various places around the dig. The Volunteers are from all walks of life, dinosaur buffs. Three or four of them have CHILDREN with them, and the kids run around, like in a giant sandbox.

Grant, Ellie, and a Volunteer walk down the hill. Grant spots a KID kicking dirt onto one of the digs. He notices and frowns.

> **GRANT**
> What's that kid doing?
>
> (to the Kid)
>
> What are you doing there!? Excuse me! Can you just back off? This is very fragile! Are you out of your mind?
>
> Get off that and go find your parents!
>
> (to Ellie)
>
> Did you see what he just did?

The Kid stomps away, pissed off.

> **KID**
> Asshole.
>
> **GRANT**
> (to Ellie)
>
> Why do they have to bring their kids?!

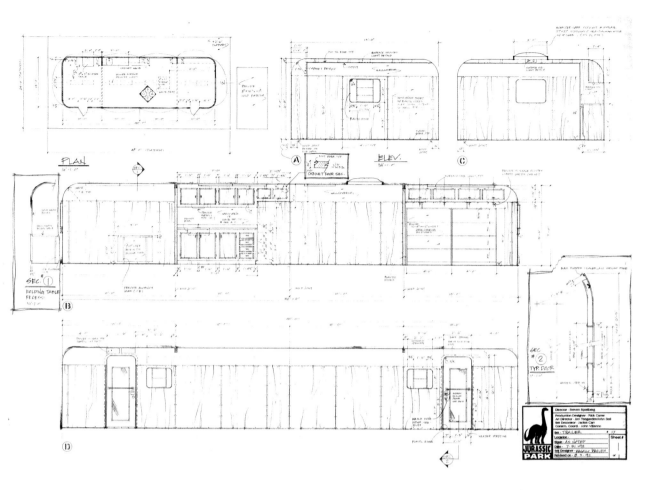

ELLIE
You could hire your help. But there's four summers of work here, with the money for one. And you say it's a learning experience, sort of a vacation, and you get volunteers with kids.

He and Ellie arrive to where several VOLUNTEERS are clustered around a computer terminal that's set up on a table in a small tent, its flaps lashed open.

GRANT
(to the Volunteer) Ready to give it a shot, Jerry?

A LITTLE GIRL moves a little too close to the machine.

ELLIE
Want to watch the computer?

Ellie quietly moves her out of Grant's way, to a place she can see.

VOLUNTEER
Thumper ready?

MAN
Ready.

VOLUNTEER
Fire.

ABOVE A construction diagram for the Grant's trailer set.

The Volunteer throws a switch on a machine that looks a bit like a floor buffer. The whole thing hops up into the air as it drives a soft lead pellet into the earth with a tremendous force. There is a dull THUD, the earth seems to vibrate, and all eyes turn to the computer screen - -

                    ELLIE
        How long does this usually take?

                  VOLUNTEER
        It should be immediate return. You
        shoot the radar into the ground,
        the bone bounces back . . .

The screen suddenly comes alive, yellow contour lines tracing across it in three waves, detailing a dinosaur skeleton.

                  VOLUNTEER
        This new program's incredible! A few
        more years of development and you
        don't have to dig anymore!

Grant looks at him, and his expression is positively wounded.

                    GRANT
        Well, where's the fun in that?

                  VOLUNTEER
        It looks a little distorted, but I
        don't think that's the computer.

                    ELLIE
              (shakes her head)

        Postmortem contraction of the
        posterior neck ligaments.

                (to Grant)

        Velociraptor?

                    GRANT
        Yes. Good shape, too. Five, six feet
        high. I'm guessing nine feet long.

        Look at the - -

He points to part of the skeleton, but when his finger touches the screen the computer BEEPS at him and the image changes. He pulls his hand back, as if it shocked him.

                  VOLUNTEER
             What'd you do?

                    ELLIE
        He touched it. Dr. Grant is not
             machine compatible.

                    GRANT
        They've got it in for me.

The Volunteer LAUGHS and touches a different part of the screen, which brings the original image back. Grant continues, but doesn't get as close.

                    GRANT
        Look at the half-moon shaped bone
        in the wrist. No wonder these guys
             learned to fly.

The group laughs. Grant is surprised.

                 GRANT (cont'd)
        Now, seriously. Show of the hands.
        How many of you have read my book?

Everyone stops laughing and looks away. Ellie raises her hand supportively. So does the Volunteer. Grant SIGHS.

                 GRANT (cont'd)
        Great. Well maybe dinosaurs have
        more in common with present-
        day birds than reptiles. Look at
        the pubic bone - - it's turned
        backwards, just like a bird. The
        vertebrae - - full of hollows and
        air sacs, just like a bird. Even the
        word raptor means "bird of prey."

The Kid steps forward and looks at the computer skeleton critically.

> KID
> That doesn't look very scary. More like a six-foot turkey.

Everyone sort of draws in their breath and steps aside, revealing the Kid, standing alone. Grant turns to the Kid, lowers his sunglasses, and stares at him like he just came from another planet.

Grant strolls over to the Kid, puts his arms around his shoulders in a friendly way.

> GRANT
> Try to imagine yourself in the Jurassic Period.

> (or)

> Try to imagine yourself in the Cretaceous Period.

Ellie rolls her eyes.

> ELLIE
> (under her breath)

> Here we go.

> GRANT
> You'd get your first look at the six-foot turkey as you move into a clearing.

But the raptor, he knew you were there a long time ago. He moves like a bird; lightly, bobbing his head. And you keep still, because you think maybe his visual acuity's based on movement, like a T-rex, and he'll lose you if you don't move. But no. Not VELOCIRAPTOR. You stare at him, and he just stares back. That's when the attack comes - - not from the front, no, from the side, from the

CAMP CREATOR

Both the novel and various screenplay drafts give little information on Grant's facilities at Snakewater, Montana. In order to research the set he would need to build for the sequence, production designer Rick Carter paid a visit to Jack Horner's real dig site in Montana. When Carter arrived at the airport, the paleontologist arrived to greet him with a friend, the legendary actor Peter Fonda. "And so I got to go out and spend a camp night with Peter Fonda and Jack Horner," Carter recalls. "In the movie *Easy Rider*, there is a very famous campsite scene where you've got Peter Fonda and Dennis Hopper—who would be like Jack and Peter—and then the third person is actually Jack Nicholson. So I was kind of the Jack Nicholson character in the middle!"

other two raptors you didn't even know were there.

Grant walks around the Kid.

> GRANT (cont'd)
> Velociraptor's a pack hunter, you see, he uses coordinated attack patterns, and he's out in force today. And he slashes at you with this - -

He takes the claw from his pocket and holds it at the front of the raptor's three-toed foot.

GRANT (cont'd)
- - a six-inch retractable claw, like
a razor, on the middle toe. They don't
bother to bite the jugular, like a
lion, they just slash here, here - -

He points to the Kid's chest and
thigh.

DIGGING FOR DINOSAURS

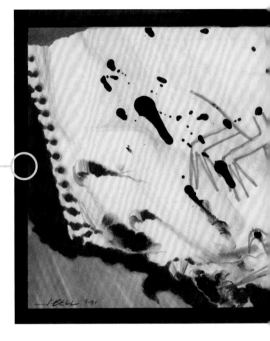

The excavation scene that introduces Grant and Sattler in the film always existed in one form or another throughout the various script drafts, having originated in Crichton's novel. In the book, Grant is first glimpsed at the Montana dig site in the hundred-degree heat, brushing away fragments of the skeleton of a baby carnivore. In Crichton's first draft, Grant's introduction sees him surrounded by "attractive college students," working together to uncover a skeleton that is eventually revealed to be a *Velociraptor*. The author's revised draft retains this introduction, although adds in an element from the novel that would be dropped in subsequent iterations: Grant and Sattler receive a fax from New York Tropical Disease Lab of a drawing of the "lizard" that bit the young vacationer, Tina, their expertise called on to identify the creature. In Scotch Marmo's draft, Grant and Sattler's expertise is showcased in a different way, when, after discovering a mild stress fracture in the right calcaneus of a raptor skeleton they have unearthed, they speculate on dinosaur behavior. Says Grant, "This animal had a vertical leap of about twelve feet. Not as entertaining as fiction, but absolutely fact without prejudice." This line would set up the raptors' athletic abilities in the mind of the audience, an idea that Koepp evolved further, writing a speech in which Grant explains the predatory skills of the *Velociraptors*. The raptors' ability to capture their prey through intelligent coordination will later be demonstrated when the dinosaurs hunt and kill the park's gamekeeper, Robert Muldoon.

In Koepp's first draft, Grant's speech is directed to an "INTERN" who believes the raptor "doesn't look very fearsome." This was changed to the "KID" in the final draft, the revised scene prefiguring the fact that two other children, Tim and Lex, will be facing these creatures for real in their grandfather's park. Grant's line from the novel "I hate computers" also made it through various iterations. In Koepp's final draft, Grant says it before joining the volunteers as they experiment with a radar used to discover dinosaur bones deep beneath the dig site. He accidentally makes the computer beep angrily at him, leading Sattler to joke: "Dr. Grant is not machine compatible." And with that he walks back across the camp, returning to his skeleton. Sattler hurries to catch up with him.

GRANT (cont'd)
- - or maybe across the belly,
spilling your intestines. Point is,
you're alive when they start to
eat you. Whole thing took about
four seconds.

The Kid is on the verge of tears.

GRANT (cont'd)
So, you know, try to show a little
respect.

ELLIE
You know, if you really wanted to
scare the kid you could've just
pulled a gun on him.

GRANT
Yeah, I know, you know . . . kids.
You want to have one of those?

ELLIE
Well, not one of those, well yeah,
possibly one at some point could be
a good thing. What's so wrong
with kids?

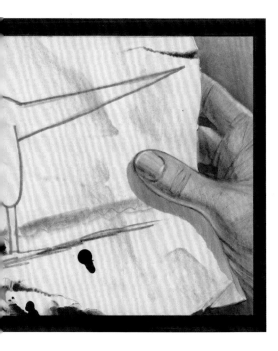

ALAN AND ELLIE

The Grant/Sattler relationship evolved considerably from the novel, in which Ellie Sattler is engaged to another man—"a nice doctor in Chicago," as Grant tells the inquisitive Tim. "The Crichton screenplays showed them just as work partners," says Scotch Marmo, whose draft includes a romantic relationship between Grant and Sattler. "The screen direction shows Alan often attracted to Ellie's smarts and humor but unable to show it directly to her. On the first helicopter ride into Jurassic Park, Ellie is asleep, her head falls on Alan's shoulder to Alan's discomfort. In the final escape scene in the helicopter, Alan is huddled close to Ellie and he puts his arm around her shoulder. She reaches and pulls it closer. Clearly a progression in their relationship and Alan is changed, he is way more open to a relationship and demonstrates it."

Koepp continued this dynamic, his final draft including an affectionate moment where Sattler takes Grant's hat off and gives him a playful hug before she kisses him. The scene was shot but didn't make it to the film, which Koepp feels was the right decision: "They're clearly a couple and they have been, one assumes, for some time. But not all couples are terribly affectionate in public with one another. And it seemed to really go with his slightly grumpy personality. That's very personal—that's the last thing he's going to do in public."

                    GRANT
      Oh, Ellie, look. They're noisy,
     they're messy, they're sticky,
            they're expensive.

                    ELLIE
          Cheap, cheap, cheap.

                    GRANT
             They smell.

                    ELLIE
      Oh my god, they do not! They
             don't smell.

                    GRANT
   They do smell. Some of them smell . . .
            babies smell.

                    ELLIE
      Alright, the one on the airplane
    had an accident, but usually babies
             don't smell.

                    GRANT
      They know very little about the
    Jurassic Period; they know less

              about the Cretaceous.

                    ELLIE
              The what?

                    GRANT
          The Cretaceous.

                    ELLIE
      Anything else, you old fossil?

                    GRANT
      Yeah, plenty. Some of them can't
                walk!

                    ELLIE
    It frustrates me so much that I love
      you, that I need to strangle you
              right now!

    Ellie playfully takes Grant's hat
    off and gives him a tight hug.
    They kiss.

ABOVE Concept art created by John Bell depicts Tina's drawing of the dinosaur that attacked her, one that is faxed over to Grant and Sattler to identify. The sequence was dropped from later drafts of the script.

GRAND ENTRANCE

In Crichton's novel, Grant is visited at his Montana dig site by Bob Morris, from the San Francisco office of the Environmental Protection Agency (EPA). Investigating the Hammond Foundation, which has been funding Grant's research to the tune of $30,000 annually for the past five years, Morris reveals that the company has been mysteriously stockpiling amber and has bought up the Costa Rican island of Isla Nublar—or "Cloud Island" as it's also known. Considered superfluous, the scene didn't make any of the screenplay drafts. In the novel, Hammond telephones Grant shortly afterward, asking about Morris's visit, and then requests Grant and Sattler travel to his "biological preserve" to offer their opinion on the site.

Before reaching the screen, the invitation scene went through a number of permutations. In Crichton's drafts, it's Hammond's legal counsel Donald Gennaro who arrives at the dig site via chopper and convinces Grant and Sattler to travel to Costa Rica with Hammond on his private jet. Scotch Marmo dropped the idea of bringing Gennaro to Montana and didn't include the Hammond phone call either. Instead, in her draft, the deal has already been struck offscreen, with Grant and Sattler receiving $60,000 in funding to visit "some resort of Hammond's in Costa Rica," as Sattler puts it, with a limousine arriving to ferry them to Hammond's helicopter. It's only in Koepp's drafts that Hammond personally arrives at the dig site via helicopter to convince them to fly to Jurassic Park.

A strange wind seems to be whipping up. Grant and Ellie look around, confused. The wind is getting stronger, blowing dirt and sand everywhere, filling in everything they've dug out, blowing the protective canvasses off. Now there's a more familiar ROAR, and they look up and see it - -

- - a huge helicopter, descending on the camp.

> ELLIE
> (to the Volunteers)
>
> Get some canvasses and cover anything that's exposed!

Grant's already on it, trying desperately to protect the skeleton he's excavating. He looks up at the helicopter and SHOUTS, shaking his fist.

CUT TO:

EXT BASE CAMP - DAY
Down at the base camp, the helicopter has landed. The PILOT is already out, waiting as GRANT comes down from the mountaintop like Moses steaming. Grant gestures wildly at him to turn the chopper off.

The Pilot points timidly to a mobile home across the camp. Grant runs to the trailer.

EXT TRAILER - DAY
The door to the trailer SLAPS open, and GRANT storms in.

> GRANT
> What the hell do you think you're doing in here?

The trailer serves as the dig's office. There are several long wooden tables set up, every inch covered with bone specimens that are neatly laid out, tagged, and labeled.

Farther along are ceramic dishes and crocks, soaking other bones in acid and vinegar.

There's old dusty furniture at one end of the trailer, and a refrigerator. A man roots around in the refrigerator, his back to us. GRUMBLING about the contents which are mostly beer.

His hand falls across a bottle of expensive champagne in the back.

                    MAN
              Ah hah!

He pulls it out - the cork POPS.

The Man turns around. JOHN HAMMOND, seventy-ish, is sprightly as hell, with bright, shining eyes that say "Follow me!"

Grant stares incredulously at the Man, holding his champagne bottle without an invitation.

                   GRANT
         Hey, we were saving that!

                  HAMMOND
         For today, I guarantee it.

                   GRANT
      And who in God's name do you think
               you are . . . ?

                  HAMMOND
       John Hammond. And I am delighted to
      finally meet you in person, Dr. Grant.

Grant is struck silent. He shakes his hand, staring dumbly.

                   GRANT
         Mr. - - Hammond?

ABOVE Champagne moment: Billionaire entrepreneur John Hammond (Sir Richard Attenborough) convinces Grant and Sattler to inspect his park.

OPPOSITE LEFT John Hammond (Attenborough), right, personally invites Dr. Alan Grant (Sam Neill) to Isla Nublar, a story point that was created in the Koepp drafts.

Hammond looks around the trailer approvingly, at the enormous amount of work the bones represent.

HAMMOND
I can see my fifty thousand a year has been well spent.

The door SLAPS open again and ELLIE comes in, just as pissed off as Grant was.

ELLIE
Okay, who's the jerk?

GRANT
Uh, this is our paleobotanist, Dr. Ellie . . .

ELLIE
Sattler.

Grant
Dr. Sattler. Ellie, this is Mr. HAMMOND. (in case she didn't catch it)

John Hammond.

ELLIE
Did I say jerk?

HAMMOND
I'm sorry for the dramatic entrance, but I'm in a hurry. Will you have a wee bit of a drink now and then?

Hammond begins to walk into the kitchen, making himself at home. Ellie follows him and tries to help. Grant settles behind the table.

HAMMOND (cont'd)
Come along then, don't let it get warm!

(expansively)

Come on in, both of you.
Sit down.

As Hammond moves, they notice he walks with a slight limp and uses a cane - - for balance or style, it's hard to say which.

ELLIE
I have samples all over the kitchen.

(she takes some stones out of one of the glasses)

HAMMOND
Come along. I know my way around a kitchen. Come along.

Ellie goes around towards Grant. She grabs a bottle of water.

They look at each other, really taken aback by this guy's bravado, and sit down. Hammond dries the glasses.

HAMMOND (cont'd)
Well now, I'll get right to the point. I like you. Both of you. I can tell instantly with people; it's a gift.

(new subject)

I own an island. Off the coast of Costa Rica. I leased it from the government and spent the last five years setting up a kind of biological preserve down there. Really spectacular. Spared no expense. It makes the one I had in Kenya look like a petting zoo. No doubt that sooner or later our attractions will send (drive the) kids right out of their minds.

GRANT
And what are those?

ELLIE
Small versions of adults, honey.

He gives her a dirty look.

JOHN HAMMOND

The John Hammond seen in Steven Spielberg's film is very different than the one who appears in the pages of Michael Crichton's novel. Although Alan Grant remarks in the book that "John Hammond's about as sinister as Walt Disney," he soon learns that the creator of Jurassic Park is in fact a mercenary capitalist: Hammond has no intention of opening the park to just anyone—only to those who can afford it. "A costly price tag actually increases the appeal of the park," he argues. Over the course of Crichton's story, Hammond becomes an increasingly embittered, angry, isolated figure, unconcerned with the safety of others, as his money-making dream begins to crumble.

Yet Spielberg did not see Hammond this way. "Steven wanted a sunnier captain of the Jurassic ship; he was clear about that," says Scotch Marmo, who admits that she and Spielberg "had very different ideas" about Hammond. "I felt that Hammond was quite insane but hid it beautifully through tact and an old-world elegance. I thought he was insane because he made a park that had raptors and *T. rexes* in it and still he brought his grandchildren to it before it had a real safety check. He took his own grandchildren to a potentially lethal park to use them as pawns . . . He had a childlike delight in what he created but he also had a Dr. Frankenstein about him. He played God and he failed." When Koepp took over, Spielberg wanted the writer to model the character on Walt Disney. "Once he became a more of a Walt Disney–like figure, he became someone who may have some very human flaws, but malevolence is not one of them," adds Koepp. The casting of Sir Richard Attenborough also helped define this softer version of the character, the revered actor imbuing Hammond with an avuncular demeanor that belied the character's overweening ambition and recklessness.

HAMMOND
Not just kids - - for everyone. We're going to open next year. Unless the lawyers kill me first. I don't care for lawyers. You?

GRANT
I, uh, don't really know any. We - -

HAMMOND
Well, I'm afraid I do. There's one, a particular pebble in my shoe. He represents my investors. He says they insist on outside opinions.

GRANT
What kind of opinions?

HAMMOND
Not to put a fine point on it, your kind. Let's face it, in your particular field, you're the top minds. If I could just get you two to sign off on the park - - you know, give a wee testimonial - - I could get back on schedule - -

ABOVE LEFT Early concept art by John Bell depicting John Hammond in his Montana dig site outfit.

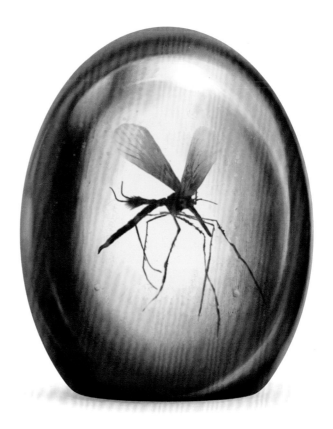

HAMMOND (cont'd)
(he Americanizes his pronunciation)

- - schedule.

ELLIE
Why would they care what we think?

GRANT
What kind of park is it?

HAMMOND
(smiles)

Well, it's - - right up your alley.

(hands Grant a drink)

Look, why don't you both (the
pair of you) come on down for the
weekend. Love to have the opinion of

a paleobotanist as well.

(hands Ellie a drink)

I've got a jet standing by at
Choteau.

(he jumps up and sits on the
counter)

GRANT
No, I'm sorry, that wouldn't be
possible. We've just discovered a
new skeleton, and - -

HAMMOND
(pours himself a drink)

I could compensate you by fully
funding your dig - -

GRANT

- - this would be an awfully unusual
time - -

HAMMOND

For a further three years.

Grant OOFS as Ellie elbows him hard
in the ribs.

ELLIE

Where's the plane?

CUT TO:

EXT CAFE DAY
DENNIS NEDRY is in his late thirties,
a big guy with a constant smile that
could either be laughing with you or
at you, you can never tell. He sits at
a table in front of a Central American
cafe, eating breakfast.

Another Legend:
SAN JOSE, COSTA RICA

Nedry looks up and sees a man get
out of a taxi - - LEWIS (Louis)
DODGSON, fiftyish, wearing a large
straw hat and looking almost too much
like an American tourist. Dodgson
clutches an attaché case close to him
and scans the cafe furtively.

Nedry laughs, shakes his head, and
waves to him.

NEDRY

Dodgson!

Dodgson hurries over to the table.

DODGSON

(as he sits)

You shouldn't use my name.

NEDRY

Dodgson, Dodgson. (loud)

We got Dodgson here! See, nobody
cares. Nice hat. What are you trying
to look like, a secret agent?

Dodgson ignores that, sets his
attaché case down next to the
table, and slides it towards Nedry.

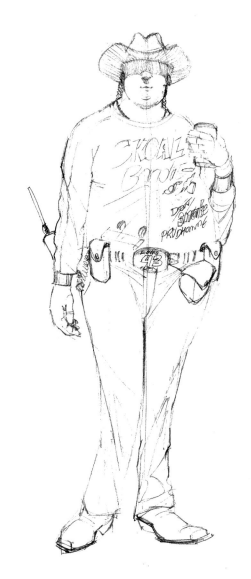

IN THE CAN

Crichton's novel sees Nedry instructed to steal embryos from Hammond's facility, with Dodgson handing him a cunningly adapted can of Gillette Foamy shaving cream in which to store the stolen goods. Scotch Marmo took a different approach, however, with Nedry instructed to steal dinosaur eggs from the incubation room. In her draft, once stowed on supply ship the *Anne B*, the eggs begin to crack. "I thought eggs were very visual," she says. "The eggs could visually escalate quite nicely: just eggs, then rocking eggs, then a crack, then a strange little dinosaur hand reaching . . . we could advance time visually and create tension and great interest—what crazy danger is in those shells?"

Koepp later returned to Crichton's original idea, although, for the final film, art director John Bell instead selected a red, blue, and white-colored Barbasol shaving foam can as the embryo receptacle.

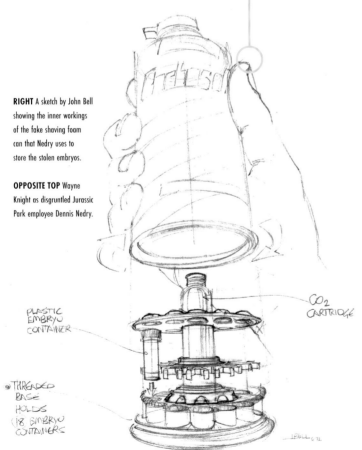

RIGHT A sketch by John Bell showing the inner workings of the fake shaving foam can that Nedry uses to store the stolen embryos.

OPPOSITE TOP Wayne Knight as disgruntled Jurassic Park employee Dennis Nedry.

PLASTIC EMBRYO CONTAINER

CO2 CARTRIDGE

THREADED BASE HOLDS (18 EMBRYO CONTAINERS

JBELL 6 72

> **DODGSON**
> Seven fifty.

Nedry smiles and pulls the attaché closer to him.

> **DODGSON (cont'd)**
> On delivery, fifty thousand more for every viable embryo. That's one point five million. If you get all fifteen species off the island.

> **NEDRY**
> Oh, I'll get 'em all.

> **DODGSON**
> Remember - - viable embryos. They're no use to us if they don't survive.

> **NEDRY**
> How am I supposed to transport them?

Dodgson pulls an ordinary can of shaving cream from a shoulder bag he carries and sets it on the table.

> **DODGSON**
> The bottom screws open; it's cooled and compartmentalized inside. They can even check it if they want. Press the top.

Nedry presses the top of the can and real shaving cream comes out. He grins, impressed. While Dodgson talks, Nedry looks around for somewhere to wipe the shaving cream and ends up dumping it on top of someone's Jell-O on a dessert tray next to him.

> **DODGSON (cont'd)**
> There's enough coolant gas for thirty-six hours.

Nedry looks at the can.

> **NEDRY**
> What? No menthol?

DODGSON
Mr. Nedry, Mr. Nedry. The embryos
have to be back here in San Jose by
then.

NEDRY
That's up to your guy on the boat.
Seven o'clock tomorrow night, at the
east dock. Make sure he got it right.

DODGSON
I was wondering, how are you
planning to beat the security?

NEDRY
I got an eighteen minute window.
Eighteen minutes, and your company
catches up on ten years of research.

A WAITER arrives and puts the check
down on the table, between them. Nedry
looks down at it pointedly, then up at
Dodgson.

NEDRY (cont'd)
Don't get cheap on me Dodgson.

Dodgson rolls his eyes and picks up
the check.

NEDRY (cont'd)
That was Hammond's mistake.

DENNIS NEDRY

Wayne Knight's note-perfect performance as traitorous coder Dennis Nedry in Spielberg's film would make the character a fan favorite. Nedry's inclusion in the film was a given, but the size and scope of his role, and the illicit contacts he works with, went through a number of iterations.

In the novel, he's first seen at the San Francisco International Airport, where he meets Lewis Dodgson of Biosyn, the corporate rival to InGen. Nedry is not even named in this first encounter, simply referred to as "a man," which amps up the cloak-and-dagger nature of their rendezvous. Crichton removed this off-island encounter in his screen adaptations. His first draft introduces Nedry as a passenger on the jet that brings Grant, Sattler, and Malcolm to Isla Nublar. The revised draft jettisons that idea entirely, and Nedry doesn't appear until he meets the tour party in the park's Control Room. In both drafts, without the meeting with Dodgson, it's unclear who is paying Nedry to betray Hammond.

This wasn't the case in Scotch Marmo's draft, which removes Dodgson and replaces him with Bill Baker, a "businessman" who works at Biogen (an invention of the writer's, not to be confused with the Crichton-created Biosyn). Scotch Marmo calls Baker a "plant" in her script, brought up early in the story to suggest that "bad things are afoot—an evil greedy man may be working against Jurassic Park—so that the audience can expect a pay-off." In this version, the two conspirators meet in a boardroom and their encounter is a fractious one, concluding with Baker punching Nedry when he tries to renegotiate his deal. The computer programmer then meets the tour party on Hammond's helicopter, traveling to Isla Nublar. In Koepp's drafts, Dodgson was reinstated, however, and his meeting with Nedry was moved to a café in San José, Costa Rica.

MANE MAN

While Malcolm was described in the novel as "a tall, thin, balding man of thirty-five," the casting of Jeff Goldblum, who boasted a thick raven-colored mane, spun the look of the character in a different direction. One thing remained consistent. "Dressed entirely in black: black shirt, black trousers, black socks, black sneakers," wrote Crichton in the book, his all-dark apparel remained intact for the finished film.

EXT OPEN SEA - DAY
A helicopter, "IN-GEN CONSTRUCTION" emblazoned on the side, skims low over the shimmering Pacific.

EXT HELICOPTER - DAY
GRANT, ELLIE, GENNARO, and MALCOLM are huddled in the back of the chopper; HAMMOND is in the front with the PILOT.

There are two other passengers as well - - DONALD GENNARO, the lawyer from the amber mine, now dressed in safari clothes, everything straight from Banana Republic. The other Dr. IAN MALCOLM, fortyish, dressed all in black, with snakeskin boots and sunglasses. Malcolm, who finds it hard to take his eyes off Ellie, leans over and SHOUTS over the engine whine.

                    MALCOLM
        So you two dig up dinosaurs?

                    GRANT
               Try to!

Malcolm laughs, finding this very amusing, which confuses Grant. Hammond turns around annoyed.

                    HAMMOND
        You'll have to get use to Dr. Malcolm! He suffers from a deplorable excess of personality, especially for a mathematician!

                    MALCOLM
        Chaotician, actually! Chaotic Dr. Ian!

Hammond SNORTS, not even bothering to cover his contempt for Malcolm.

OPPOSITE Jeff Goldblum as chaotician Dr. Ian Malcolm, a character that only became a lock for the final film when the actor was cast in the role.

BELOW LEFT An early sketch by John Bell conceptualizes chaos theorist Dr. Ian Malcolm, complete with hand tattoo featuring a radioactive symbol.

IAN MALCOLM

Chaos theorist Dr. Ian Malcolm endured a rough ride during the development of the screenplay. Although Crichton deemed him worthy of including in his two drafts, Scotch Marmo felt the need to drop Malcolm from hers. "*Jurassic Park* had so many moving parts to it that adding Malcolm felt like overweighting an already complex action story," she says. "I had to make people believe the science was real, that Alan and Ellie found the island believable, that Hammond was a mad visionary, and the reason for bringing everyone together was to tour the park to assure the investors it was safe. And so much more . . . everything had to break down. Malcolm felt like one more large element that may overstock the story."

Koepp's first draft also excised the character. "Honestly, it was because it was too hard," he admits. "If you read the book, he talks a lot. He talks about math a lot, and he talks and abstracts a lot. And I just couldn't figure out how to make it visual. I couldn't figure out how to. And I thought about all sorts of things." At one point, Koepp thought he had made a breakthrough, taking inspiration from Errol Morris's 1991 documentary *A Brief History of Time*. Based on the famed book by Stephen Hawking, it visualized some of the physicist's theories through graphics, something Koepp considered for Malcolm. "I thought, 'Okay, well, maybe when he's talking, we start to see what he's talking about in visual terms.' And Steven said, 'No, because if I do it once, then I have to do it throughout the movie, because it's a style thing. And that's not the kind of style I want to have.'" It was at this point that Jeff Goldblum read for the Malcolm role, deeply impressing Spielberg. "He had Jeff Goldblum come in, and just read some stuff from the book. And he said, 'He was so great, you got to put him in, this guy will play it great.' So then I worked a little harder, which I think is all he was asking me to do."

MALCOLM

John doesn't subscribe to
Chaos, particularly what it
has to say about his little
science project!

HAMMOND

Codswallop! Dr. Ian, you've never
come close to explaining these
concerns of yours about this island!

MALCOLM

I certainly have! Very clearly!
Because of the behavior of the
system in phase space!

Hammond just waves him off.

HAMMOND

A load, if I may say so, of
fashionable number crunching, that's
all it is!

MALCOLM

(poking at Hammond's knee)

John, John.

HAMMOND

(pushing him away)

Don't do that!

MALCOLM

Dr. Grant, Dr. Sattler - - you've
heard of Chaos Theory?

ELLIE

(shaking her head)

No.

MALCOLM

No? Non-linear equations? Strange
attractions?

(again, she shrugs)

Dr. Sattler, I refuse to believe
that you are not familiar with the
concept of attraction!

Grant just rolls his eyes as Malcolm
gives her an oily grin, but Ellie
smiles, enjoying Grant's jealousy.
Hammond turns to Gennaro and gives
him a dirty look.

HAMMOND

I bring scientists - - you bring a
rock star.

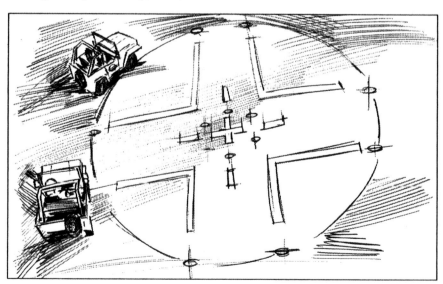

OPPOSITE TOP A John
Bell concept sketch of
the InGen helicopter.

RIGHT A storyboard panel
featuring the helipad and two
waiting Jurassic Park jeeps.

Hammond looks out the windshield, and CLAPS his hands excitedly.

> HAMMOND
> There it is!

Up ahead, the others see it.

ISLA NUBLAR. It's a smallish island, completely ringed by thick clouds that give it a lush, mysterious feel. The PILOT pulls up over a spot in the clouds and starts to descend, fast.

> HAMMOND (cont'd)
> Bad wind shears! We have to drop pretty fast! Hold on, this can be a little thrilling!

The helicopter drops like a stone. Outside the windows, they can see cliff walls racing by, uncomfortably close. They bounce like hell, hitting wild up and down drafts.

Only Hammond still feels chatty.

> HAMMOND (cont'd)
> We're planning an airstrip! On pilings, extending out into the ocean twelve thousand feet! Like La

ROUGH LANDING

Crichton's drafts indicated the helicopter's fraught arrival on Isla Nublar, buffeted "wildly in the thermals," but this idea evolved further in later script iterations. "My draft elaborated the danger of the helicopter landing to foreshadow that technology is on the brink of losing control," says Scotch Marmo. She depicts the chopper "violently" shaking, which concerns the passengers, including Nedry, whose hand "crushes a packet of crackers," sending his lunch flying. Koepp retained the helicopter's turbulent descent to its helipad, although the bumpy ride is not nearly as fraught as Scotch Marmo's concept.

Guardia, only a lot safer! What do you think?

They don't answer, just hold on. As they near the ground, a luminous white cross appears below them, a landing pad shining through the Plexiglas bubble in the floor of the chopper.

The cross grows rapidly larger as the chopper plummets, but a sudden updraft catches them and they bounce skyward for a moment then drop again, even faster if possible, before landing with a hard BUMP.

EXT HELICOPTER LANDING PAD - DAY

The chopper plummets and finally lands. One of the WORKERS opens the door and the GROUP gets out. HAMMOND looks out, proudly.

EXT HILLTOP - DAY

Two large, open-top jeeps ROAR down the hilltop away from the landing cross as the helicopter engines WHINE back to life and the rotors start to spin again.

ELLIE, GRANT, and MALCOLM hold on tight in the front jeep,

HAMMOND and GENNARO are in the rear jeep. Both cars have DRIVERS.

They pass through an enormous gate in a thirty foot high fence, which is closed behind them by two PARK ATTENDANTS.

There are large electrical insulators on the fences, warning lights that strobe importantly and clear signs - - "ELECTRIFIED FENCE! 10,000 VOLTS!"

IN THE REAR JEEP,

THESE PAGES Storyboards depict the tour vehicles bringing John Hammond's guests into the park for their first look at living, breathing dinosaurs.

Gennaro regards the fences critically.

> #### GENNARO
> The full fifty mile of perimeter fence are in place?

> #### HAMMOND
> And the concrete moats, and the motion sensor tracking systems. Donald, dear boy, do try to relax and enjoy yourself.

> #### GENNARO
> Let's get something straight, John. This is not a weekend excursion, this is a serious investigation of the stability of the island. Your investors, whom I represent, are deeply concerned. Forty-eight hours from now, if they - -
>
> (gestures to Grant, Ellie, and Malcolm)
>
> - - aren't convinced, I'm not convinced. And I can shut you down John.

> #### HAMMOND
> Forty-eight hours from now, I'll be accepting your apologies. Now get out of the way. So I can see them!

He shoves Gennaro aside, to get a clear view of Grant, Ellie, and Malcolm.

> #### HAMMOND (cont'd)
> I wouldn't miss this for the world.

The jeeps wind their way along a mountain road.

IN THE LEAD JEEP,

Ellie stares off to the right, fascinated by the thick tropical plant life around them. She tilts her head, as if something's wrong with this picture.

She reaches out and grabs hold of a leafy branch as they drive by, TEARING it from the tree.

IN THE REAR JEEP,

Hammond watching Grant, signals to his Driver.

> HAMMOND
> Just stop here, stop here. Slow, slow.

He slows down, then stops. So does the front jeep.

IN THE FRONT JEEP,

Ellie stares at the leaf, amazed, running her hand lightly over it.

> ELLIE
> Alan - -

But Grant's not paying attention. He's staring too, out the other side of the jeep.

Grant notices that several of the tree trunks are leafless - just as thick as the other trees, but gray and bare.

> ELLIE (cont'd)
> (still staring at the leaf)
>
> This shouldn't be here.

Grant twists in his seat as the jeep stops and looks at one of the gray tree trunks. Riveted, he slowly stands up in his seat, as if to get

closer. He moves to the top of the seat, practically on his tiptoes.

He raises his head, looking up the length of the trunk. He looks higher.

And higher.

And higher.

That's no tree trunk. That's a leg. Grant's jaw drops, his head falls all the way back, and he looks even higher, above the tree line.

> ELLIE (cont'd)
> (still looking at the leaf)
>
> This species of vermiform has been extinct since the cretaceous period. This thing - -

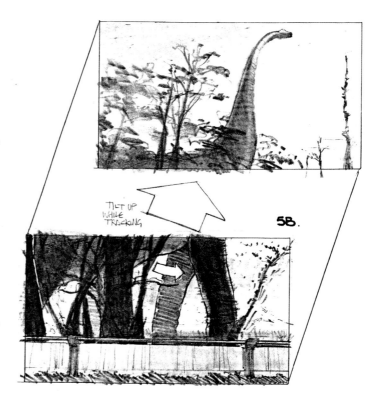

THESE PAGES The tour party gets close to the *Brachiosaurs* in these evocative storyboards.

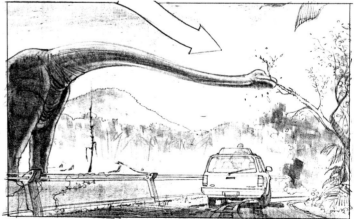

Grant, never tearing his eyes from the brachiosaur, reaches over and grabs Ellie's head, turning it to face the animal.

She sees it, and drops the leaf.

>   ELLIE (cont'd)
>   Oh - - my - - God.

Grant lets out a long, sharp, HAH - a combination laugh and shout of joy.

He gets out of the jeep, and Ellie follows. Grant points to the thing and manages to put together his first words since its appearance:

>   GRANT
>   THAT'S A DINOSAUR!

- - a dinosaur. Chewing the branches. Technically, it's a brachiosaur, of the sauropod family, but we've always called it brontosaurus. It CRUNCHES the branch in its mouth, which is some thirty-five feet up off the ground, at the end of its long, arching neck. It stares down at the people in the car with a pleasant, stupid gaze.

Ellie looks up at the sauropods in wonder.

They're pretty light on their feet - a far cry from the sluggish, lumbering brutes we would have expected.

Hammond gets out of his jeep and comes back to join them. He looks like a proud parent showing off the kid.

Dr. Ian Malcolm looks at Hammond, amazed, and with an expression that is a mixture of admiration and rapprochement.

FIRST CONTACT

In the novel, the first dinosaur that Grant, Sattler, and the others meet is a *Brontosaurus*, glimpsed shortly after they land on Isla Nublar. Crichton adjusted this in his first draft: "TWO GIGANTIC APATOSAURS rumble away." However, at the suggestion of Phil Tippett, the species was changed to a bigger, more imposing sauropod, the *Brachiosaurus*. In Scotch Marmo's draft, there are two *Brachiosaurs*, though she shifted the encounter to be at the start of the tour itself, with Grant even fainting at the sight of the dinosaurs. "I wanted to hold it back because I thought the reveal would be that much more euphoric for the audience and justify Dr. Grant fainting," she says. "Steven respected my idea of maximizing the mounting of the tension—I think he went back and forth on it too."

In Koepp's first draft, he pared down the encounter scene to feature just one *Brachiosaurus*, comparing it to "an oversized giraffe." Creating the scene itself took a masterful combination of on-set special effects, CG techniques, and a little imagination on set. Shot on Kualoa Ranch, a privately owned four-thousand-acre site, the live action footage was captured using very basic in-camera special effects. To ensure that the actors had an eyeline reference during the sequence, a fifty-foot pole with a foam dinosaur head was used as a stand-in for the *Brachiosaurus*. Then, to create the moment where the dinosaur eats leaves from the top of a tall tree, a large crane was connected to the tree with cables, so the operator could pull at it and shake the branches. The *Brachiosaurus* was created later by Industrial Light & Magic.

"ELLIE, WE CAN TEAR UP THE RULE BOOK ON COLD-BLOODEDNESS."
– ALAN GRANT

                    MALCOLM
        You did it. You crazy son of a bitch,
                    you did it.

Grant and Ellie continue walking,
following the dinosaur.

                    GRANT
              The movement!

                    ELLIE
        The - - agility. You're right!

In their amazement, Grant and Ellie
talk right over each other.

                    GRANT
        Ellie, we can tear up the rule book
              on cold-bloodedness.

        It doesn't apply, they're totally
          wrong! This is a warm-blooded
        creature. They're totally wrong.

ELLIE

They were wrong. Case closed. This thing doesn't live in a swamp to support its body weight for God's sake!

Several of the top branches are suddenly RIPPED away. Another sauropod, reaching for a branch high above their heads, stands effortlessly on its hind legs.

GRANT

(to Hammond)

That thing's got a what, twenty-five, twenty-seven foot neck?

HAMMOND

The brachiosaur? Thirty.

Grant and Ellie continue to walk.

GRANT

- - and you're going to sit there and try to tell me it can push blood up a thirty-foot neck without a four-chambered heart and get around like that?! Like that!?

(to Hammond)

This is like a knockout punch for warm-bloodedness.

HAMMOND

(proudly)

We clocked the T-rex at thirty-two miles an hour.

ELLIE

You've got a T-rex!?

(to Grant)

He's got a T-rex! A T-rex! He said he's - -

GRANT

Say again?

HAMMOND

Yes, we have a T-rex.

Grant feels faint. He sits down on the ground.

WELCOME TO JURASSIC PARK!

When it comes to famous lines in movie history, John Hammond's "Welcome to Jurassic Park!" delivered with typical vigor by Sir Richard Attenborough, is right up there. What is even more remarkable, though, is that in Koepp's first draft, that line was given to Ed Regis. "Seems impossible to imagine now!" remarks Koepp, who switched the line to Hammond when he cut Regis from the story during later revisions.

ABOVE A storyboard shows the arrival of the jeep at a Jurassic Park vista.

OPPOSITE TOP "They do move in herds": John Hammond, Dr. Ellie Sattler, and Dr. Alan Grant marvel at the majesty of Jurassic Park.

OPPOSITE RIGHT An early storyboard, depicting *Parasaurolophus* in a Jurassic Park lake.

                    ELLIE
          Honey, put your head between your
                knees, and breathe.

Hammond walks in front of them and
looks out.

                   HAMMOND
          Dr. Grant, my dear Dr. Sattler.
             Welcome to Jurassic Park.

They turn and look at the view
again. It's a beautiful vista,
reminiscent of an African plain. A
whole herd of dinosaurs crosses the
plain, maybe a hundred that we see
in a quick glance alone.

                    GRANT
          Ellie, they're absolutely - -
             they're moving in herds.

          They do move in herds!

                    ELLIE
              We were right!

                    GRANT
                 (to Hammond)

          How did you do it?!

                    (or)

          How did you do this?!

HAMMOND
I'll show you.

Finally, we notice Gennaro, who was sort of faded into the background while the others reacted. He's just staring, a look of absolute rapture on his face.

He speaks in a voice that is hushed and reverent.

GENNARO
We are going to make a fortune with this place.

EXT MAIN COMPOUND - DAY

The main compound of Jurassic Park
is a large area with three main
structures connected by walkways
and surrounded by two impressive
fences, the outer fence almost
twenty feet high.

Outside the fences, the jungle has
been encouraged to grow naturally.

The largest building is the
visitor's center, several stories
tall, its walls still skeletal,
unfinished. There's a huge glass
rotunda in the center.

The second building looks like a
private residence, a compound unto
itself, with smoked windows and its
own perimeter fence.

The third structure isn't really a
building at all, but the impressive
cage we saw earlier, overgrown
inside with thick jungle foliage.
The jeeps pull up in front of the
visitor's center.

EXT VISITOR'S CENTER - DAY

HAMMOND leads GRANT, ELLIE, GENNARO,
and MALCOLM up the stairs, talking
as he goes. Two ladies open the
doors to the Visitor Center.

INT VISITOR'S CENTER - DAY

The lobby of the still-unfinished
visitor's center is a high-
ceilinged place, and has to be
to house its central feature, a
large skeleton of a tyrannosaur
that is attacking a bellowing
sauropod. WORKMEN in the basket of
a Condor crane are still assembling
skeletons. A staircase climbs the
far wall, to another wing.

ABOVE A storyboard panel
shows a tour vehicle entering
the gateway to Jurassic Park.

OPPOSITE Another John
Bell conceptual drawing for
the Jurassic Park entrance,
described in the script as
"enormous, primitive gates,
torches blazing on either side."

EXTINCTION REBELLION

Another of *Jurassic Park*'s most memorable lines went through a number of revisions. In Scotch Marmo's script, Grant, having witnessed real dinosaurs for the first time after a lifetime of digging up their remains, says to Ellie: "We're the ones that are extinct now." By the time the story had evolved into Koepp's final draft, the line had been moved to the party's arrival at the Visitor Center after witnessing the *Brachiosaurus*. Sattler asks Grant what he's thinking. "We're out of a job," replies the paleontologist, to which Malcolm pithily responds, "Don't you mean 'extinct'?" It was a line paraphrased from a conversation that Phil Tippett had with Spielberg, after the animator learned that the director was abandoning Go-Motion animation and switching to groundbreaking digital techniques.

"He [Spielberg] laid down the edict that it was all going to be done with computer graphics. He asked me how I felt. I said, 'I felt like Georges Méliès! . . . I feel extinct.' He went, 'That's great, I'm putting that in the movie!'" Although Tippett was disappointed with the news, he went on to become a key figure in the production. "Phil Tippett simply switched his role from the craft of creating, one frame at a time, Go-Motion dinosaurs, literally to becoming the director of the behavior of all the animals," says Spielberg. Credited as dinosaur supervisor, Tippett ensured the CG animations were grounded in real-life anatomical principles so that the movement of the dinosaurs felt natural and realistic.

                    HAMMOND
                  (continuing)

- - the most advanced amusement park
  in the world, combining all the
latest technologies. I'm not talking
rides, you know. Everybody has rides.
We made living biological attractions
 so astonishing they'll capture the
   imagination of the entire planet!

GRANT stares up at the dinosaur
skeletons and just shakes his head.
ELLIE catches his reaction.

                    ELLIE
        So what are you thinking?

                    GRANT
          We're out of a job.

Ian Malcolm pops in between them.

                   MALCOLM
        Don't you mean "extinct"?

Ellie and Malcolm move on ahead.

CUT TO:

INT SHOW ROOM - DAY

> HAMMOND
> Why don't you all sit down.

GRANT, ELLIE, and MALCOLM take their seats in the front row of the fifty seat auditorium. GENNARO sits behind them. HAMMOND walks over to the giant screen in front of them.

Behind him, a huge image of himself beams down at him from the giant television screen.

> HAMMOND (screen)
> Hello, John!

> HAMMOND (stage)
> (to the group)
>
> Say hello!
>
> (then, fumbling with his three by five cards)
>
> Oh, I've got lines.

He scans them, looking for his place. The screen Hammond continues without him.

> HAMMOND (screen)
> Fine, I guess! But how did I get here?!

> HAMMOND (stage)
> Uh - -
>
> (finding his place)
>
> "Here, let me show you. First I'll need a drop of blood. Your blood!"

The screen-Hammond extends his finger and the stage-Hammond reaches out and mimes poking it with a needle.

> HAMMOND (screen)
> Ouch, John! That hurt!

> HAMMOND (stage)
> "Relax, John. It's all part of the miracle of cloning!"

While the two Hammonds rattle on, the screen image splits into two Hammonds, then four then eight, and so on, like a shampoo commercial.

Grant, Ellie, and Malcolm huddle together excitely in the audience.

> GRANT
> Cloning from what?! Loy extraction has never recreated an intact DNA strand!

> MALCOLM
> Not without massive sequence gaps!

> ELLIE
> Paleo-DNA? From what source? Where do you get 100 million year old dinosaur blood?!

> GENNARO
> Shhhhh!

IN THE FILM,
the screen-Hammond is joined by another figure, this one animated. MR. DNA is a cartoon character, a happy-go-lucky double-helix strand of recombinant DNA. Mr. DNA jumps down onto the screen-Hammond's head and slides down his nose.

> HAMMOND
> Well! Mr. DNA! Where'd you come from?

> MR. DNA
> From your blood! Just one drop of your blood contains billions of strands of DNA, the building blocks of life!

OPPOSITE TOP Malcolm (Jeff Goldblum), Grant (Sam Neill), and Sattler (Laura Dern) climb the stairs of the Visitor Center lobby, where Malcolm drops the famous "Don't you mean 'extinct'?" line.

MR. DNA

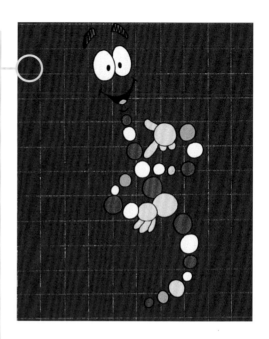

While Crichton's novel explains the science behind Hammond's dinosaurs in detail, the final film wouldn't be able to deliver the same level of exposition needed to present the key scientific info in an easy-to-understand way that would be accessible for a general audience. To achieve this, the idea of adding an introductory film to the tour scenes that would explain the science in layman's terms was explored in early versions of the script. Crichton's drafts featured Ed Regis presenting the talk and interacting with an "onscreen" version of himself, as the informative film unspools. Scotch Marmo replaced Regis with Hammond in a similar scene, calling him "an elder Carl Sagan," a nod to the American astronomer.

Later, Koepp and Spielberg began tossing around alternative ideas that would be livelier and more engaging than a lecture. From those conversations, the cartoon character Mr. DNA was born, a brightly colored figure who explains the film's complex scientific concepts in an approachable way. Spielberg said he took the idea from a series of Frank Capra directed science documentaries he watched in school, such as 1957's *Hemo the Magnificent*, which focused on the workings of the circulatory system and featured animated elements. "It was a live action movie, but it had an animated character in it, Hemo, and he would tell you all about blood. And I remember he had an accent for some reason,"[2] says Koepp, who wrote Mr. DNA with a Jamaican burr in his first draft, an idea later dropped. The animation for the character was created by Bob Kurtz, the founder of Kurtz & Friends, an animation studio based in Burbank, who would later go on to work on Spielberg's *Minority Report*. Actor Greg Burson—who in 1989 had taken over voicing Bugs Bunny following the death of original Bugs actor Mel Blanc—voiced Mr. DNA, giving the character a friendly, southern gentleman vibe.

2   *Scriptnotes*, Episode 418, "The One with David Koepp," September 26, 2019

ABOVE RIGHT The character of Mr. DNA, as seen in the animated info film created by Bob Kurtz.

OPPOSITE Mr. DNA explains how a prehistoric mosquito unlocked secrets to the genetic rebirth of the dinosaurs in these images from the animated informational film.

IN THE FILM,
Mr. DNA has taken over the show, and is speaking to the audience from the screen.

> **MR. DNA**
> A DNA strand like me is a blueprint
> for building a living thing!
> And sometimes animals that went
> extinct millions of years ago, like
> dinosaurs, left their blueprints

> behind for us to find! We just had to
> know where to look!

The screen image changes from animated to a nature-photography look. It's an extreme close-up of a mosquito, its fangs suck deep into some animal's flesh, its body pulsing and engorging with the blood it's drinking.

> **MR. DNA (cont'd)**
> A hundred million years ago, there
> were mosquitoes, just like today.
> And, just like today, they fed
> on the blood of animals. Even
> dinosaurs!

The camera races back to show the mosquito is perched on top of a giant animated brachiosaur.

The image changes, to another close-up, this one of a tree branch, its bark glistening with golden sap. Mr. DNA leaps on the sap.

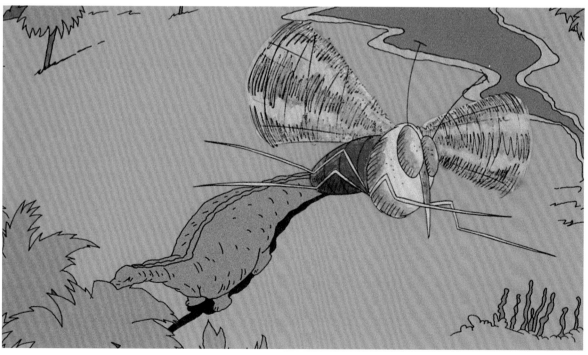

MR. DNA (cont'd)
    Sometimes, after biting a
dinosaur, the mosquito would land
  on a branch of a tree, and get
          stuck in the sap!

The engorged mosquito lands in the
tree sap, and gets stuck. So is
Mr. DNA. He tugs his legs, but they
stay stuck.

                MR. DNA
                WHOA!

Now the tree sap flows over them,
covering up Mr. DNA and the mosquito
completely. Mr. DNA SHOUTS from
inside the tree sap.

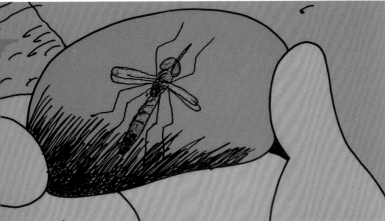

            MR. DNA (cont'd)
After a long time, the tree sap would
  get hard and become fossilized, just
 like a dinosaur bone, preserving the
            mosquito inside!

A SCIENCE LABORATORY
The place buzzes with activity.
Everywhere, there are piles of
amber, tagged and labeled with
SCIENTISTS in white coats examining
it under microscopes.

One SCIENTIST moves a complicated
drill apparatus next to the chunk
of amber with a fossilized mosquito
inside and BORES into the side of
it. MR. DNA escapes through the
drill hole as the Scientist moves
the amber onto a microscope and
peers through the eyepiece.

              MR. DNA (o.s.)
  This fossilized tree sap - - which we
call amber - waited millions of years,
   with the mosquito inside - until
Jurassic Park's scientists came along!

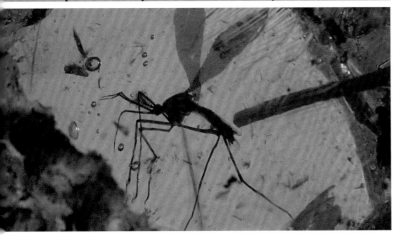

THROUGH THE MICROSCOPE
We see the greatly enlarged image of a mosquito through the lens.

> MR. DNA (o.s.)
> Using sophisticated techniques, they extract the preserved blood from the mosquito, and - -

A long needle is inserted through the amber, into the thorax of the mosquito, and makes an extraction.

> MR. DNA (cont'd)
> - - Bingo! Dino DNA!

Mr. DNA jumps down in front of DNA data as it races by at headache speed. He holds his head, dizzied by it.

> MR. DNA (cont'd)
> A full DNA strand contains three billion genetic codes! If we looked at screens like these once a second for eight hours a day, it'd take two years to look at the entire strand!

It's that long! And since it's so old, it's full of holes! That's where our geneticists take over!

INT GENETICS LAB - DAY
SCIENTISTS toil in a lab with two huge white towers at either side.

> MR. DNA
> Thinking Machine supercomputers and gene sequencers break down the strand in minutes - -

One SCIENTIST, in the back has his arms encased in two long rubber tubes. He's strapped into a bizarre apparatus, staring into a complex headpiece and moving his arms gently, like Tai Chi movements.

> MR. DNA (cont'd)
> - - and Virtual Reality displays show our geneticists the gaps in the DNA sequence! Since most animal DNA is ninety percent identical, we use the complete DNA of a frog - -

OPPOSITE In these images from the informational film, John Hammond's scientists extract blood from a mosquito, perfectly preserved in amber.

LEFT An animated frog seen in the informational film represents the use of frog DNA to fill in gaps in dinosaur DNA, a methodology that will have major implications for Jurassic Park.

ON THE V.R. DISPLAY

we see an actual DNA strand, except it has a big hole in the center, where the vital information is missing. Mr. DNA bounds into the frame, carrying a bunch of letters in one hand.

He puts it in the gap and turns his back against it, GRUNTING as he shoves it into place.

> MR. DNA
> (straining)

– – to fill in the – – holes and – – complete – – the – –

> (finally getting it)

– – code! Whew!

He brushes his hands off, satisfied.

> MR. DNA (cont'd)
> Now we can make a baby dinosaur!

IN THE AUDIENCE

The scientists look at each other, not sure.

> HAMMOND
> All this has some dramatic music – – da dum da dum da dum dum – – march or something, it's not written yet, and the tour moves on – –

He throws a switch and safety bars appear out of nowhere and drop over their seats, CLICKING into place.

> HAMMOND
> For your own safety!

The row of seats moves out of the auditorium.

INT HALLWAY DAY

The row of seats moves slowly past a row of double-paned glass windows beneath a large sign that reads "GENETICS/FERTILIZATION/ HATCHERY." Inside, TECHNICIANS work at microscopes.

ABOVE Understanding DNA: Spielberg took the idea for the informational film from the science documentaries he saw in school.

OPPOSITE The animated informational film visualizes the hatching of a dinosaur, complete with DNA strand.

In the back is a section entirely lit by blue ultraviolet light. Mr. DNA's VOICE continues over a speaker in each seat.

                    MR. DNA (o.s.)
   Our fertilization department is
   where the dinosaur DNA takes the
place of the DNA in unfertilized emu
or ostrich eggs - - and then it's on
to the nursery, where we welcome the
   dinosaurs back into the world!

GENNARO has a wondrous grin plastered on his face, just loving everything now.

                    GENNARO
   This is overwhelming, John.
   Are these characters (people)
            animatronics?

                    HAMMOND
   No, we don't have any animatronics
   here. These are the real miracle
      workers of Jurassic Park.

GRANT, ELLIE, and MALCOLM are frustrated, leaning forward, straining against the safety bars for a better look. But the cars keep going.

                    GRANT
   Wait a minute! How do you interrupt
         the cellular mitosis?!?

                    ELLIE
   Can't we see the unfertilized host
                eggs?!

But the cars are already moving on to another set of windows, which give a glimpse into what looks like a control room.

                    HAMMOND
      Shortly, shortly . . .

                    MR. DNA (o.s.)
   Our control room contains some of
   the most sophisticated automation
         ever attempted in - -

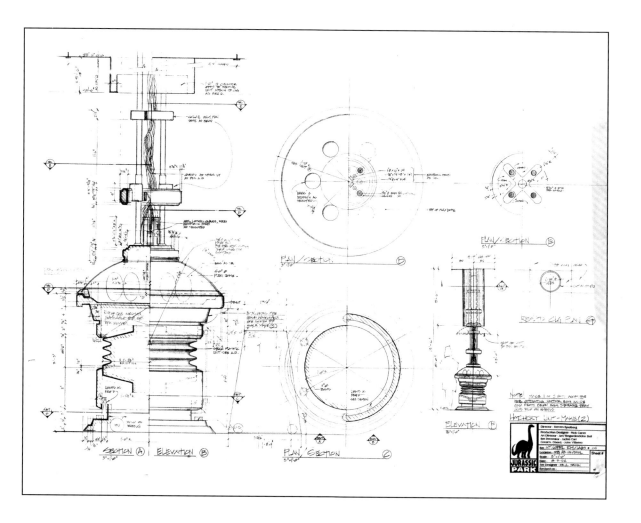

Grant strains to look back into the labs, but the cars move past again, no intention of slowing down.

> **GRANT**
> Can't you stop these things?!

> **HAMMOND**
> Sorry! It's kind of a ride!

> **GRANT**
> (to Malcolm)
>
> Let's get outta here!

The two of them team up on the safety bars. Grant shoves his all the way back with one foot and Malcolm does the same. They stand up and head for the door of the hatchery.

> **GENNARO**
> Hey! You can't do that!

Too late. Ellie slips out from under her safety bar too and stomps right across Gennaro's seat.

ABOVE An incubator blueprint.
OPPOSITE Baby *Triceratops* concept by Mark "Crash" McCreery.

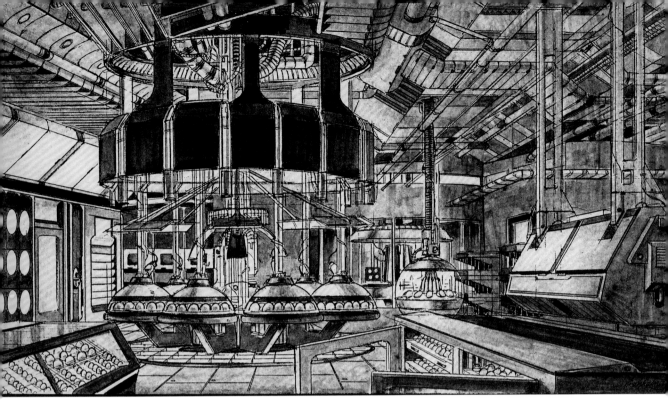

ABOVE An early concept
sketch by Tom Cranham of
the Jurassic Park breeding
laboratory, including
several incubators.

OPPOSITE BOTTOM
Dr. Henry Wu (B.D. Wong)
is the chief geneticist
of Jurassic Park.

GENNARO
Can they do that?

They reach the door to the hatchery.
Grant tries to shove it open, but
just THUDS into it. He rattles the
handle, but the door won't budge as
it's on a security key-card system.

HAMMOND steps up and takes his
glasses off.

HAMMOND
Relax, Donald, relax. They're
scientists. They ought to be
curious.

(he steps up to the code box)

It's a retinal scanner.

He pushes various code numbers. The
door opens. He steps aside, and the
group eagerly goes up the stairs.

INT HATCHERY/NURSER - DAY
The hatchery is a vast, open room,
bathed in infrared light.

Long tables run the length of the
place, all covered with eggs, their
pale outlines obscured by hissing low
mist that's all through the room.

HAMMOND
Come on in.

HAMMOND takes off his hat and hands
it to one of the TECHNICIANS.

HENRY WU, late twenties, Asian-
American, wearing a white lab coat
works at a nearby table, making notes.

HAMMOND (cont'd)
Good day, Henry.

WU
Oh, good day, Sir.

GRANT goes to a round, open
incubator with various eggs under
a strong light.

One of the eggs makes strong movements -
a robotic arm steadies the shell.

GRANT

My God! Look!

Hammond, ELLIE, and MALCOLM join
him, as does Henry Wu.

WU

Ah, perfect timing! I'd hoped they'd
hatch before I had to go to the boat.

HAMMOND

Henry, why didn't you tell me? You
know I insist on being here when
they're born.

DR. HENRY WU

Dr. Henry Wu, John Hammond's chief geneticist, is only featured in one sequence in Koepp's final draft, taking questions from the excited tour party in his lab and overseeing the hatching of a baby raptor. In the novel, he has a larger role, in which he butts heads with Hammond over genetic alterations to the park's dinosaurs, arguing that they should be modified to meet the public's expectations. Wu also meets a grim fate in the book, gruesomely torn apart by a *Velociraptor* at Hammond's lodge. Both Crichton and Scotch Marmo carried Wu's death over into their drafts, but Koepp ultimately spared the character. "I think, in general, more people die in the book than in the movie. The tone we wanted to hit was slightly different," says Koepp. Ironically, even though Dr. Wu, played by actor B.D. Wong, would only be featured in one *Jurassic Park* scene, he would become a fan favorite character, with Wong returning in a more substantial role for the Jurassic World trilogy and even featuring in the animated series *Camp Cretaceous*.

INSIDE PLAYPEN: OVER THE CREATURE WRAPPED IN A TOWEL. TIM COMES FORWARD AS A TECHNICIAN GOES TO GREET THE GROUP (MORE)

Hammond puts on a pair of plastic gloves.

The egg begins to crack. The robotic arm moves away . . . a BABY DINOSAUR tries to get out, just its head sticking out of the shell.

Hammond reaches down and carefully breaks away egg fragments, helping the baby dinosaur out of its shell.

                    HAMMOND
        Come on, then, out you come.

                HAMMOND (cont'd)
        They imprint on the first living
        creature they come in contact
        with. That helps them to trust me.
        I've been present for the birth of
        every animal on this Island.

            Just look at that.

                    MALCOLM
        Surely not the ones that have bred
                in the wild?

                    WU
        Actually, they can't breed in the
        wild. Population control is one of our
        security precautions here. There is no
        unauthorized breeding in Jurassic Park.

Grant and Ellie exchange a look. She manages not to smile.

                    MALCOLM
        How do you know they can't breed?

                    WU
        Because all the animals in Jurassic
            Park are females. (I've) We
            engineered them that way.

Hammond keeps his attention trained on the new dinosaur.

3Ⓒ

CONTINUES: BOOM UP AS TIM IMPULSIVELY OPENS
THE LID OF THE PLAY PEN (MORE)

3Ⓓ

CONTINUES: THE BABY RAPTOR LEAPS
TO THE RAIL AND LOOKS AT TIM.

HAMMOND
There you are. Out you come.

ELLIE
Oh my God.

HAMMOND
Could I have a tissue please?

WU
Right away (certainly). Coming right up.

The animal is now free, Hammond sets it down carefully next to its shell. Grant picks it up and holds it in the palm of his hand, under the incubator's heat light.

GRANT
Blood temperature feels like high eighties.

HAMMOND
Wu?

WU
Ninety-one.

Grant picks up the large, broken half-shell, but the robotic arm snatches it back out of his hand, and puts it down.

GRANT
Homeothermic? It holds that temperature?

(to Wu)

Incredible.

Malcolm is looking at Hammond, skeptical.

MALCOLM
But again, how do you know they're all female? Does someone go into the park and, uh - - lift up the dinosaurs' skirts?

OPPOSITE Tim and Grant examine the newborn baby raptor in these storyboards.

LEFT John Hammond (Richard Attenborough) greets a newborn raptor.

LIFE FINDS A WAY

In Koepp's final draft, Dr. Ian Malcolm addresses Dr. Wu's arrogant assertion that the dinosaurs in the park are all female and therefore cannot breed: "I'm simply saying that life . . . finds a way." The roots of what became one of the most famous lines in not just *Jurassic Park*, but the subsequent franchise, can be found in the novel, in which Malcolm says: "Life breaks free. Life expands to new territories. Painfully, perhaps even dangerously. But life finds a way. I don't mean to be philosophical but there it is." Koepp later featured the same phrase in his script for *Jurassic Park*'s sequel *The Lost World* (1997), when Hammond tells Malcolm about Isla Sorna, a secret site where exhibits were bred for the park that has since been overrun by the dinosaurs. "Life will find a way, as you once so eloquently put it," Hammond says. Explains Koepp, "I used it in the second movie as a sort of callback to the first movie, and I think, at that point, it became the theme of the entire series." The phrase "life finds a way" later became the tagline for the fifth installment, *Jurassic World: Fallen Kingdom* (2018).

WU

We control their chromosomes. It's not that difficult. All vertebrate embryos are inherently female anyway. It takes an extra hormone at the right developmental stage to create a male, and we simply deny them that.

HAMMOND

Your silence intrigues me.

MALCOLM

John, the kind of control you're attempting is not possible. If there's one thing the history of evolution has taught us, it's that life will not be contained.

Life breaks free. It expands to new
territories. It crashes through
barriers. Painfully, maybe even . . .
dangerously, but and . . . well,
there it is.

Ellie listens to him, impressed.

                    HAMMOND
          Watch her head - support
               her head.

Grant, ignoring the others, picks
up the baby dinosaur, and holds it
on the palm of his hand, under the
incubator's heat light. He spreads
the tiny animal out on the back
of his hand and delicately runs
his finger over its tail, counting
the vertebrae. A look of puzzled
recognition crosses his face.

                      WU
          You're implying that a group
          composed entirely of females will
                    breed?

                   MALCOLM
     I'm simply saying that life - - finds
               a way.

                    ELLIE
          "You can't control anything." I
          agree with that. I like that.

She walks over to Malcolm, he smiles
at her, too warmly.

               ELLIE (cont'd)
     You can talk. I don't know how to
     say it. You're just articulate. You
     say everything that I think, that I
          feel. It's exciting.

                    (or)

     I find it so exciting. It's exciting
     that you can't control life, that
          you know - -

                    (or)

You know that, I find it terrifying.
     Life will always find a way.

                   MALCOLM
     That's right. Will break through.

                    ELLIE
               I get ah - -

                   MALCOLM
     I know, it's very exciting.

                    ELLIE
               And scary.

                   MALCOLM
               And scary.

                    ELLIE
When people try to control things
     that are out of their power - -

                   MALCOLM
          It's anti-nature.

                    ELLIE
               Anti-nature.

Grant doesn't notice, as he's
still obsessed with the infant
dinosaur, measuring and weighing it
on a nearby lab bench. He stops, a
strange look on his face. He knows
what this animal is - - but it
can't be.

                    GRANT
          (dreading the answer)

          What species is this?

                      WU
     Uh - - it's a Velociraptor.

Grant and Ellie turn slowly and look
at each other, then look at Hammond,
astonished.

                    GRANT
          You bred raptors?

EXT RAPTOR PEN - DAY

GRANT charges across the compound, a fire in his eyes, ahead of ELLIE, MALCOLM, and GENNARO. HAMMOND struggles to keep up.

> **HAMMOND**
> Dr. Grant, Dr. Grant? Uh - - we planned to show you the raptors later, after lunch.

But Grant has stopped abruptly next to the Velociraptor pen, which we recognize as the heavily fortified cage we saw earlier, with the San Quentin tower at one end.

Grant stands right up against the fence, eyes wide, dying for a glimpse.

Hammond catches up, slightly out of breath.

> **HAMMOND (cont'd)**
> Dr. Grant - - as I was saying, we've laid out lunch for you before you head out into the park. Alejandro, our gourmet chef - -

> **GRANT**
> What are they doing?

As they watch, a giant crane lowers something large down into the middle of the jungle foliage inside the pen. Something very large.

It's a steer. The poor thing looks disconcerted as hell, helpless in a harness, flailing its legs in the air.

> **HAMMOND**
> Feeding them.
>
> (moving along)

ABOVE An early concept drawing for the raptor pen by artist John Bell.

OPPOSITE TOP An unfortunate cow is lowered into the raptor pen in this storyboard panel.

OPPOSITE BOTTOM (*Left to right*) Hammond (Richard Attenborough), Gennaro (Martin Ferrero), Grant (Sam Neill), Malcolm (Jeff Goldblum), and Sattler (Laura Dern) watch feeding time at the raptor pen.

Alejandro is preparing a delightful meal for us. A Chilean sea bass, I believe. Shall we?

Grant goes up to the viewing deck. The others follow, staring as the steer disappears into the shroud of foliage. The line from the crane hangs for a moment.

The jungle seems to grow very quiet. They all stare at the motionless crane line. It jerks suddenly, like a fishing pole finally getting a nibble. There's a pause - -

- - and then a frenzy. The line jerks every which way, the jungle plants sway and SNAP from some frantic activity within, there is a cacophony of GROWLING, of SNAPPING, of wet CRUNCHES that mean the steer is literally being torn to pieces and it almost makes it worse that we can't see anything of what's going on - -

(5) MULDOON FIRES AND BARELY ESCAPES

PENNED IN

In a scene taken directly from the novel, Crichton's first draft sees Grant, Ellie, Malcolm, and Tim arrive at the park's raptor pen to witness the ferocity of these pack hunters. In the first draft, three raptors are seen charging at the electric fence, but in Crichton's second draft, he reduced the number to two, with Hammond and Dr. Wu featuring in the scene rather than the guests. In Scotch Marmo's version, Hammond and Muldoon feature, with the gamekeeper informing his boss that one of the raptors tunneled free and maimed an unnamed individual: "He ripped a boy's arm off before I could get a bullet in him."

Rather than showing the raptors, Scotch Marmo's version was more subtle, with the only glimpse of the creatures being "a dark claw" holding onto the electrified fence and causing a shower of sparks. In Koepp's version, the scene was altered to feature a cow being lowered into the pen at feeding time, the ravenous raptors that tear the unfortunate creature apart entirely unseen. While the decision to keep the raptors offscreen at this stage in the story further stokes the tension, according to Rick Carter it was purely a pragmatic decision. "Each one of those raptor shots was $50,000 at that time," says Carter. Needing to spend the budget wisely, it made more sense to show the foliage in the pen violently shake back and forth, suggesting that the raptors are descending upon the cow. "It's like a piranha scene in a James Bond movie, where you bring up whatever was lowered into the water, and it's gone," adds Carter.

- - and then it's quiet again. The line jerks a few times, then stops. Slowly the SOUND of the jungle starts up again.

                    HAMMOND
          Fascinating animals, fascinating.

                    ELLIE
               Oh my God.

                    HAMMOND
          Give time, they'll out draw the
               T-rex. Guarantee it.

                    GRANT
          I want to see them. Can we get
                    closer?

Ellie puts a hand on his arm, like calming an overexcited child.

                    ELLIE
          Alan, these aren't bones anymore.

                    HAMMOND
     We're - - still perfecting a viewing
     system. The raptors seem to be a bit
     resistant to integration into a park
                    setting.

A VOICE comes from behind them.

                 VOICE (o.s.)
          They should all be destroyed.

They turn and look at the man who spoke. ROBERT MULDOON, the grim-faced man who was present at the accident in the beginning, is fortyish, British.

He joins them and takes his hat off. When Muldoon talks, you listen.

                    HAMMOND
          Robert. Robert Muldoon, my game
          warden from Kenya. Bit of an
     alarmist, I'm afraid. But he's dealt
     with the raptors more than anyone.

ROBERT MULDOON

In Crichton's novel, Jurassic Park's gamekeeper Robert Muldoon is described as "a big man, fifty years old, with a steel-gray moustache and deep blue eyes." According to the author's backstory, Muldoon was raised in Kenya and has spent most of his life as a guide for African big-game hunters. "What I liked about Muldoon is that he was in such stark contrast to the others," says Koepp. "There were a couple bleeding heart scientists, a thoughtful yet rapacious businessman. And this bizarre mathematician of the likes we've never seen before. So to throw a hunter in there with them was really fun. It's contrasting styles—you really get people to play off each other." Although in Crichton's novel it's indicated that Muldoon has a drinking problem ("You're drunk," Ellie says to him at a vital moment), that was never a part of his characterization for the film. While Crichton's revised draft sees Arnold warn Hammond about the danger presented by the raptors, both Scotch Marmo's and Koepp's drafts assign this dialogue to Muldoon, giving him a steely edge and showing that he was not afraid to stand up to his employer. To play the role, Spielberg cast Bob Peck, an acclaimed British actor known for his BAFTA-winning turn as a police officer in the BBC thriller *Edge of Darkness*.

OPPOSITE Muldoon faces a raptor attack in this early storyboard panel.

ABOVE LEFT British actor Bob Peck, cast as Jurassic Park gamekeeper Robert Muldoon.

LEFT A storyboard shows the "prey" being lowered to its doom in the raptor pen.

"PREY": SHAKES & JERKS AS IT RISES.

GRANT
(introducing himself)

Alan Grant. Tell me, what kind of
metabolism do they have? What's
their growth rate?

(or)

rate of growth.

MULDOON
They're lethal at eight months. And
I do mean lethal. I've hunted most
things that can hunt you, but the
way these things move - -

GRANT
Fast for biped?

MULDOON
Cheetah speed. Fifty, sixty miles
per hour if they ever got out in
the open. And they're astonishing
jumpers.

HAMMOND
Yes, yes, yes, which is why we take
extreme precautions. The viewing
area below us will have eight-inch
tempered glass set in reinforced
steel frames to - -

GRANT
Do they show intelligence?
With the brain cavity like theirs
we assumed - -

MULDOON
They show extreme intelligence, even
problem solving. Especially the big
one. We bred eight originally, but
when she came in, she took over the
pride and killed all but two of the
others. That one - - when she looks
at you, you can see she's thinking
(or) working things out. She's the
reason we have to feed 'em like
this. She had them all attacking the
fences when the feeders came.

THESE PAGES Storyboards
depicting a sequence connected
to Crichton's second draft
in which Hammond and Dr.
Wu visit the pen, and one
of the raptors throws itself
at the electrified fence.

ELLIE
The fences are electrified, right?

MULDOON
That's right. But they never attack
the same place twice. They were
testing the fences for weaknesses.
Systematically. They remembered.

Behind them, the crane WHIRRS
back to life, raising the cable
back up out of the raptor pen.
The guests turn and stare as
the end portion of the cable
becomes visible. The steer has
been dragged completely away,
leaving only the tattered, bloody
harness. Hammond CLAPS his hands
together excitedly.

HAMMOND
Who's hungry? After you, my dear.

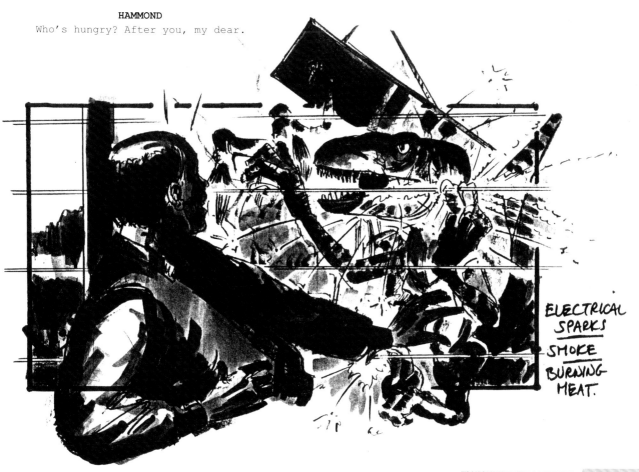

ELECTRICAL
SPARKS
SMOKE
BURNING
MEAT.

INT VISITOR CENTER PRESENTATION ROOM - DAY

HAMMOND, GRANT, ELLIE, MALCOLM, and GENNARO eat lunch at a long table in the visitor's center restaurant.

There is a large buffet table and two WAITERS to serve them.

The room is darkened and Hammond is showing slides of various scenes all around them. Hammond's own recorded voice describes current and future features of the park while the slides flash artists' renderings of all of them.

The real Hammond turns and speaks over the narration.

BELOW An early sketch of the Visitor Center by *Jurassic Park* art director, Jim Teegarden.

OPPOSITE TOP John Hammond (Richard Attenborough) hosts his guests for lunch, and a rather uncomfortable discussion about the park's ethics.

HAMMOND
None of these attractions have been finished yet. The park will open with the basic tour you're about to take,

and then other rides will come on line after six or twelve months. Absolutely spectacular designs. Spared no expense.

More slides CLICK past, a series of graphs dealing with profits, attendance, and other fiscal projections. Donald Gennaro, who has become increasingly friendly with Hammond, even giddy, grins from ear to ear.

GENNARO
And we can charge anything we want! Two thousand a day, ten thousand a day - - people will pay it! And then there's the merchandising - -

HAMMOND
Donald, this park was not built to cater only to the super rich. Everyone in the world's got a right to enjoy these animals.

GENNARO
Sure, they will, they will.

(laughing)

We'll have a - - coupon day or
something.

Grant looks down, at the plate he's
eating from. It's in the shape of
the island itself. He looks at his
drinking cup. It's got a T-rex on
it, and a splashy Jurassic Park
logo.

There are a stack of folded
amusement park-style maps on the
table in front of Grant. He picks
one up. Boldly, across the top it
says, "Fly United to Jurassic Park!"

HAMMOND
(on tape)

- - from combined revenue streams
for all three parks should reach
eight to nine billion dollars
a year - -

HAMMOND
(to Gennaro)

That's conservative, of course.
There's no reason to speculate
wildly.

GENNARO
I've never been a rich man. I hear
it's nice. Is it nice?

Ian Malcolm, who has been watching
the screens with outright contempt,
SNORTS, as if he's finally had
enough.

MALCOLM
The lack of humility before
nature that's been displayed here
staggers me.

APPENDIX TRICKS

In Koepp's first draft, the lunch scene, where Hammond argues with his guests about the ethics of creating a dinosaur park, takes place in the lobby of the Visitor Center. In the final draft, it's moved to a presentation room where slides are being projected in the background, while Hammond's recorded voice "describes current and future features of the park." Koepp wrote material for these background recordings, which can be found in the appendix of a revised draft (dated June 30, 1992). "That was the first script where I used appendices, which I do to this day," he explains. The idea of keeping this additional dialogue at the bottom of the script, away from the scene itself, was to help the reader. "You don't want people reading it to get clogged up. And suddenly your lovely four-page dialogue scene is now six. And it just feels out of place."

In this case, the additional Hammond dialogue—snatches of which can be heard playing faintly in the finished film—is a fascinating insight into the character's ambitions for the park. "When fully operational, Jurassic Park's direct revenues from attendance and lodging alone should exceed four billion dollars a year," says Hammond, who also reveals that InGen Construction has leased a large tract of land in the Azores for Jurassic Park Europe and an island near Guam for Jurassic Park Japan. While these were details taken from the novel—in which Hammond predicted direct revenues of ten million dollars a year, and merchandising doubling that—Koepp added a neat detail: According to the voice recordings, Hammond was in negotiations with the People's Republic of China to launch Jurassic Park Beijing—"the first western enterprise to bring its profits home from China."

They all turn and look at him.

GENNARO
Thank you, Dr. Malcolm, but I think things are a little different than you and I feared.

MALCOLM
Yes, I know. They're a lot worse.

GENNARO
Now, wait a second, we haven't even seen the park yet. Let's just hold out concerns until - -

(or alt. version)

Wait - we were invited to this island to evaluate the safety conditions of the park, physical containment. The theories that all simple systems have complex behavior, that animals in a zoo environment will eventually begin to behave in an unpredictable fashion have nothing to do with that evaluation. This is not some existential furlough, this is an on-site inspection. You are a doctor. Do your job. You are invalidating your own assessment. I'm sorry, John - -

HAMMOND
Alright Donald, alright, but just let him talk. I want to hear all viewpoints. I truly do.

(or)

I truly am.

MALCOLM
Don't you see the danger, John, inherent in what you're doing here? Genetic power is the most awesome force ever seen on this planet. But you wield it like a kid who's found his dad's gun.

GENNARO
If I may . . . It is hardly appropriate to start hurling - -

MALCOLM

Excuse me, excuse me - -

GENNARO

generalizations before - -

MALCOLM

I'll tell you. The problem with the scientific power you've used is it didn't require any discipline to attain it. You read what others had done and you took the next step. You didn't earn the knowledge yourselves, so you don't take the responsibility for it. You stood on the shoulders of geniuses to accomplish something as fast as you could, and before you knew what you had, you patented it, packaged it, slapped it on a plastic lunch box, and now you want to sell it.

HAMMOND

You don't give us our due credit. Our scientists have done things no one could ever do before.

MALCOLM

Your scientists were so preoccupied with whether or not they could that they didn't stop to think if they should. Science can create pesticides, but it can't tell us not to use them. Science can make a nuclear reactor, but it can't tell us not to build it!

HAMMOND

But this is nature! Why not give an extinct species a second chance?! I mean, Condors. Condors are on the verge of extinction - - if I'd created a flock of them on the island, you wouldn't be saying any of this!

(or)

have anything to say at all!

LEFT Out to lunch: Dr. Ellie Sattler (Laura Dern) listens as Hammond argues the case for Jurassic Park.

OPPOSITE TOP Dr. Alan Grant (Sam Neill) has concerns about Hammond's biological tinkering and what it might lead to.

MALCOLM

Hold on - - this is no species that
was obliterated by deforestation or
the building of a dam. Dinosaurs had
their shot. Nature selected them for
extinction.

HAMMOND

I don't understand this Luddite
attitude, especially from a
scientist. How could we stand in the
light of discovery and not act?

MALCOLM

There's nothing that great about
discovery.

(or)

What's so great about discovery?
It's a violent, penetrative act that
scars what it explores. What you
call discovery I call the rape of
the natural world!

GENNARO

Please - - let's hear something from
the others. Dr. Grant? I am sorry - -
Dr. Sattler?

ELLIE

The question is - - how much
can you know about an extinct
ecosystem, and therefore, how could
you assume you can control it?
You have plants right here in this
building, for example, that are
poisonous. You picked them because
they look pretty, but these are
aggressive living things that have
no idea what century they're living
in and will defend themselves.
Violently, if necessary.

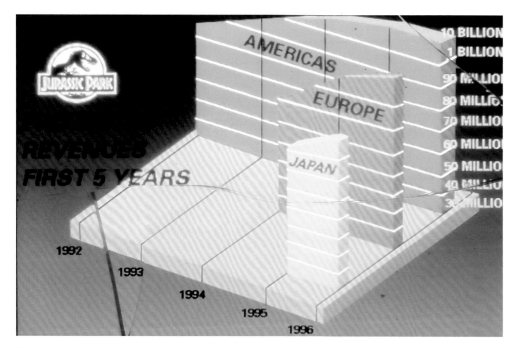

REVENUES FIRST 5 YEARS

AMERICAS
EUROPE
JAPAN

10 BILLION
1 BILLION
90 MILLION
80 MILLION
70 MILLION
60 MILLION
50 MILLION
40 MILLION
30 MILLION

1992
1993
1994
1995
1996

Exasperated, Hammond turns to Grant, who looks shell-shocked.

                    HAMMOND
Dr. Grant, if there's one person who can appreciate all of this - -

                    (or)

        What am I trying to do?

But Grant speaks quietly, really thrown by all of this.

                    GRANT
I feel - - elated and - - frightened and - -

                (starts over)

    The world has just changed so radically. We're all running to catch up. I don't want to jump to any conclusions, but look - -

He leans forward, a look of true concern on his face.

                GRANT (cont'd)
Dinosaurs and man - - two species separated by 65 million years of evolution - - have just been suddenly thrown back into the mix together. How can we have the faintest idea of what to expect?

                    HAMMOND
I don't believe it. I expected you to come down here and defend me from these characters and the only one I've got on my side is the bloodsucking lawyer!?

                    GENNARO
                Thank you.

One of the WAITERS whispers to Hammond.

                    HAMMOND
Ah - - they're here.

                    GRANT
                Who?

OPPOSITE AND ABOVE
These slides created by Caroline Quinn can be seen on the displays in the presentation room.

"YOU FOUR ARE GOING TO HAVE A LITTLE COMPANY OUT IN THE PARK."

–JOHN HAMMOND

TOP Hammond's grandchildren join the party: Lex (Ariana Richards, *far left*) and Tim (Joseph Mazzello, *far right*). Also pictured are (*left to right*) Gennaro (Martin Ferrero), Sattler (Laura Dern), and Grant (Sam Neill).

OPPOSITE TOP Lex (Richards) and Tim (Mazzello) hug grandfather John Hammond (Richard Attenborough).

OPPOSITE BOTTOM Concept art by John Bell shows a younger Lex and an older Tim.

INT VISITOR'S CENTER LOBBY - DAY
HAMMOND, GRANT, ELLIE, MALCOLM, and GENNARO walk out of the restaurant and into the lobby of the visitor's center. They head down the stairs, and pass the skeletons of the dinosaurs again.

HAMMOND
You four are going to have a little company out in the park. Spend a little time with our target audience.

Maybe they'll help you get the spirit of this place.

GRANT
What does he mean by "target audience"?

Hammond turns toward the door of the center and throws his arms out expansively.

HAMMOND
(bellowing)

KIDS!!

Two kids standing in the doorway to the center break into broad smiles. TIM, the boy, is about nine years old; ALEXIS, his sister, looks around twelve.

TIM & LEX
Grandpa!

They race across the lobby and into Hammond's arms, knocking him over on the steps.

LEX
We miss you.

TIM
Thanks for the presents.

LEX
We love the presents.

HAMMOND
You must be careful with me. Did you
like the helicopter?

TIM
It was great! It drops, we were
dropping!

Grant looks on.

TIM AND LEX MURPHY

The evolution of Hammond's grandchildren Tim and Lex is particularly fascinating. In the novel, Tim is "a bespectacled boy of about eleven" and Lex is a few years younger "perhaps seven or eight," wearing her blonde hair under a Mets baseball cap. She carries a baseball mitt slung over her shoulder—"a Darryl Strawberry special," named after the Mets player—although the glove is later lost in a *Cearadactylus* attack at Jurassic Park's aviary. Crichton ports these characterizations over into his screenplay, his first draft describing Tim, 11, as "bespectacled-scholarly, borderline-nerdy," whereas Lex is "a tomboy of 7." Lex's mitt also makes an appearance in a scene—taken straight from the novel—where she plays ball with Gennaro and almost loses her glove in a shed near the park's lagoon (here, Crichton switched the glove to become "a Kirk Gibson special," after the Detroit Tigers player). She's not so lucky in the revised draft; during the kitchen scene, a raptor tears the glove apart. The Scotch Marmo draft also continues the baseball motif: After the Main Road attack, the traumatized Lex is seen curled up in a drainpipe, her baseball glove in her mouth, rocking back and forth and banging her head against the pipe—a scene taken directly from the novel. Meanwhile, in the novel, Tim is a dinosaur enthusiast and even owns Alan Grant's book *Lost World of the Dinosaurs*, a beat Scotch Marmo includes in her draft. Koepp continued this into the final draft, with Tim noting that he has read Grant's book, the cover of which is glimpsed in the completed movie (retitled as *Dinosaur Detectives*).

By the time Koepp came on board, Spielberg had hit upon the idea of casting Joseph Mazzello, who he'd previously auditioned for *Hook*. Just eight at the time filming was due to begin, Mazzello's tender age made Spielberg realize that his onscreen sibling would need to be older, not younger, and so the production looked for an older actress to play Lex, eventually settling upon Ariana Richards, who was due to turn thirteen during the shoot. The baseball references were dropped, but Lex inherited some of Tim's "borderline-nerdy" qualities.

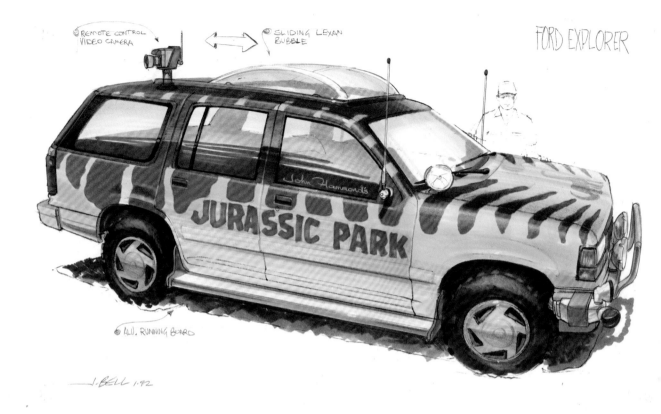

Remote control video camera

SLIDING LEXAN BUBBLE

FORD EXPLORER

John Hammond's

JURASSIC PARK

ALU. RUNNING BOARD

J. BELL 1.92

ABOVE Concept art by John Bell shows the tour vehicle, complete with animal print design and sliding roof.

OPPOSITE A cover created by the art department for Dr. Alan Grant's book *Dinosaur Detectives*.

EXT VISITOR'S CENTER - DAY
Two modified Ford Explorers leap up out of an underground garage beneath the visitor's center. They move quietly, with a faint electronic HUM, and straddle a partially buried metal rail in the middle of the road. They pull to a stop where the group is gathered.

ELLIE is off to the side with ALEXIS, introducing herself warmly.

HAMMOND is with MALCOLM, GRANT, and GENNARO.

HAMMOND
    Have a heart gentlemen. Their parents are getting a divorce and they need the diversion.

GENNARO
Hey! Where are the brakes?

HAMMOND
    Brakes? No. No brakes. They're electric cars, guided by this track in the roadway, and totally non-polluting, top of the line!

LEX
It's an interactive CD-ROM. Look, see - - you just touch the right part of the screen and it talks about whatever you want.

HAMMOND
Spared no expense. Have fun. I'll be watching you from the control (or) back in control.

(to Ellie)

Come along, my dear. You'll ride in the second car, I can promise you you'll have a real wonderful time.

ELLIE

Oh thank you so much. So I'll see you later then.

Hammond turns and heads back towards the Visitor's Center.

MALCOLM
(too eagerly; to Grant)

I'll ride with Dr. Sattler.

(or)

I'm going to ride with Dr. Sattler.

He turns and walks over to Ellie. Grant frowns, not liking this one bit. He moves to follow, but TIM cuts him off, and stares up at him, wide-eyed.

TIM

I read your book.

GRANT

Oh, yeah - - great.

Grant heads for the rear car. Tim follows.

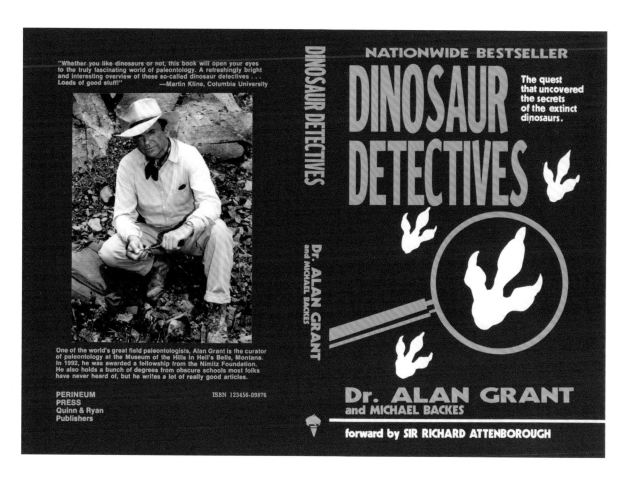

"Whether you like dinosaurs or not, this book will open your eyes to the truly fascinating world of paleontology. A refreshingly bright and interesting overview of these so-called dinosaur detectives . . . Loads of good stuff!"
—Martin Kline, Columbia University

One of the world's great field paleontologists, Alan Grant is the curator of paleontology at the Museum of the Hills in Hell's Bells, Montana. In 1992, he was awarded a fellowship from the Nimitz Foundation. He also holds a bunch of degrees from obscure schools most folks have never heard of, but he writes a lot of really good articles.

PERINEUM PRESS
Quinn & Ryan Publishers

ISBN 123456-09876

DINOSAUR DETECTIVES

NATIONWIDE BESTSELLER

DINOSAUR DETECTIVES

The quest that uncovered the secrets of the extinct dinosaurs.

Dr. ALAN GRANT
and MICHAEL BACKES

forward by SIR RICHARD ATTENBOROUGH

"I HEARD A METEOR HIT THE EARTH AND MADE LIKE THIS ONE-HUNDRED-MILE CRATER SOMEPLACE DOWN IN MEXICO . . ."

—TIM MURPHY

ABOVE Joseph Mazzello as Tim Murphy, a dinosaur superfan who is in awe of Dr. Alan Grant.

OPPOSITE Concept art by John Bell showing the interior of the Ford Explorer, complete with yellow handsets that were removed from the final design.

> **TIM**
> You really think dinosaurs turned into birds? And that's where all the dinosaurs went?

Grant opens the door of the rear car and climbs in. Tim follows.

> **GRANT**
> Well, uh, a few species - - may have evolved, uh - - along those lines - - yeah.

A mechanical voice intones from inside:

> **VOICE**
> "Two to four passengers to a car, please. Children under ten must be accompanied by an adult."

Tim is right behind Grant, so Grant keeps moving, across the back seat of the car and out the other door. But Tim follows.

> **TIM**
> Because they sure don't look like birds to me. I heard a meteor hit the earth and made like this one-hundred-mile crater someplace down in Mexico - -

> **GRANT**
> Listen, ahh - -

TIM

Tim.

GRANT

Tim. Which car were you
planning on - -

TIM

Whichever one you are.

Grant goes to the front car again,
opens the rear door, and holds it
for Tim, who climbs in the back
seat, rattling on and on.

TIM

Then I heard about this thing in OMNI?
About the meteor making all this heat
that made a bunch of diamond dust? And
that changed the weather and they died
because of the weather? Then my teacher
told me about this other book by a guy
named Bakker? And he said the dinosaurs
died of a bunch of diseases.

SLAM! Grant closes the car door on
Tim. He turns and heads for the rear
vehicle - -

- - and bumps right into Lex.

LEX
(points at Ellie)

She said I should ride with you because
it would be good for you.

Grant looks over at Ellie, annoyed.

GRANT
She's a deeply neurotic woman.

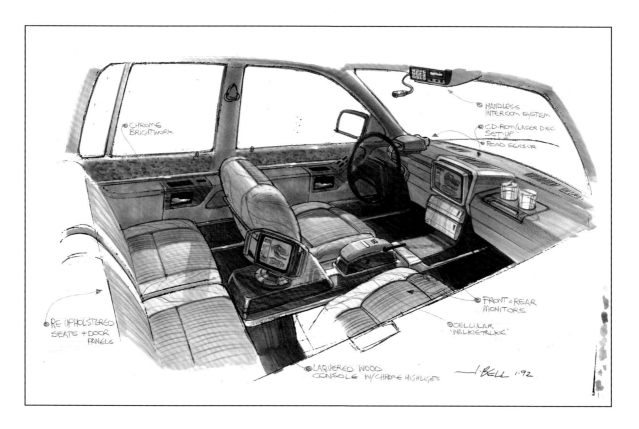

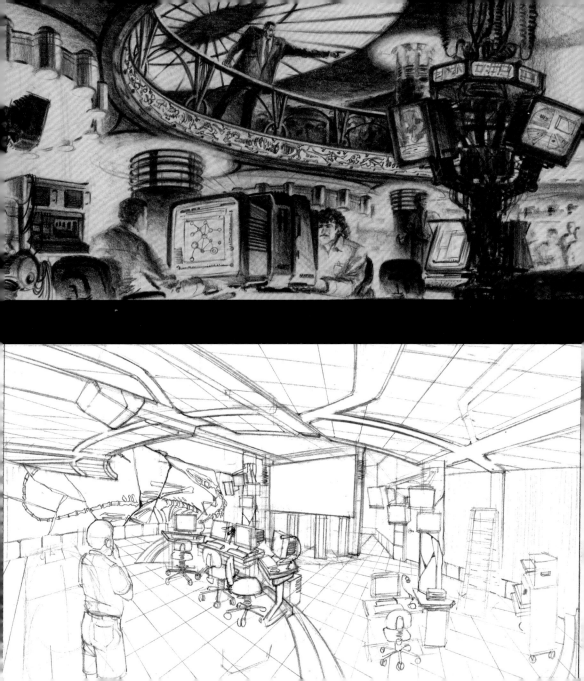

CUT TO:

INT CONTROL ROOM - DAY
The Jurassic Park control room looks like a mission control for a space launch, with several computer terminals and dozens of video screens that display images of various dinosaurs, taken from all over the park.

There's a large glass map of the island at the front of the room that is lit up like a Christmas tree with various colored lights, each one with a number and identification code next to it.

But the place is unfinished, with unattached cables, construction materials, and ladders scattered about.

The mood among the half dozen TECHNICIANS present is chaotic as they rush around with last-minute adjustments.

MULDOON whisks in through the double doors. HAMMOND is right behind him. They go straight to the main console, where RAY ARNOLD fortyish, a chronic worrier and chain-smoker, is seated.

MULDOON
National Weather Service is tracking a tropical storm about seventy-five miles west of us.

Hammond sighs and looks over Arnold's shoulder.

HAMMOND
Why didn't I build in Orlando?

MULDOON
I'll keep an eye on it. Maybe it'll swing south like the last one.

ABOVE Robert Muldoon (Bob Peck) with John Hammond (Richard Attenborough) in the Control Room.

OPPOSITE Concept sketches by John Bell that offer two very different takes on the Control Room.

                    HAMMOND
                  (a deep breath)

        Ray, start the tour program.

He punches a button on the console.

                    ARNOLD
              (not exactly comforting)

            Hold onto your butts.

CUT TO:

EXT VISITOR'S CENTER - DAY
With a loud CHUNK, the Explorers
start forward along the electrical
pathway.

GENNARO, TIM, and LEX are in the
front vehicle; GRANT, ELLIE, and
MALCOLM in the rear.

EXT MAIN GATES - DAY
They pass through two enormous,
primitive gates, torches blazing on
either side.

EXT JURASSIC PARK - DAY
IN THE REAR CAR,

the Explorer's speakers BLARE with
fanfare of trumpets, and the interior
video screen flashes "Welcome to
Jurassic Park." A familiar VOICE
comes over the speaker:

                  VOICE (o.s.)
        Welcome to Jurassic Park. You are
        now entering the lost world of the
             prehistoric past, a world - -

                  VOICE (cont'd)
        creatures long gone from the face of
        the earth, which you are privileged
               to see for the first time.

INT CONTROL ROOM - DAY
HAMMOND watches the monitor. His
grandchildren are enjoying themselves.

                    HAMMOND
        By the way, that's James Earl Jones
          (or) Richard Kiley. We spared no
                     expense!

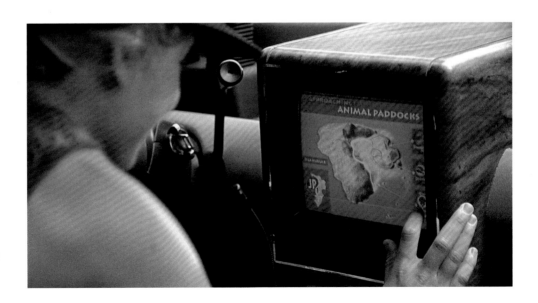

RIGHT State of the art:
Lex (Ariana Richards)
discovers the interactive
CD-ROM in the tour car.

OPPOSITE TOP Concept
art by John Bell for the
tour car interior.

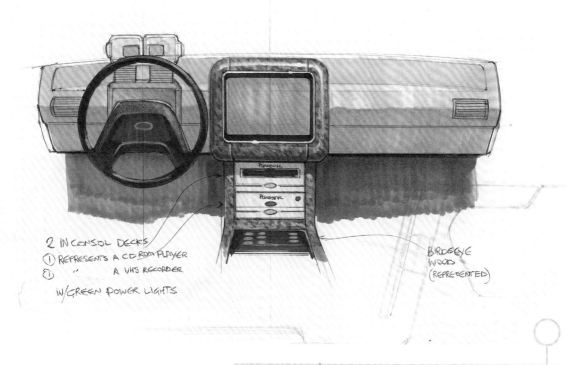

FORD EXPLORER
INSTURMENT PANEL

2 IN CONSOL DECKS
① REPRESENTS A CD-ROM PLAYER
② " A VHS RECORDER
W/GREEN POWER LIGHTS

BIRDSEYE
WOOD
(REPRESENTED)

IN THE PARK,
the fences and retaining walls are
covered with greenery and growth,
to heighten the illusion of moving
through a jungle.

IN THE FRONT CAR

GENNARO
The accident took place in a
restricted area. It would not have
been available to the public access.
So how can the safety of the public
be called into question?

The cars come to the top of a low
rise, where a break in the foliage
gives them a view down a sloping field
that is broken by a river. The tour
voice continues.

THE NARRATOR

In Crichton's novel, Tony award-winning actor Richard Kiley narrates the
tour. However, in Koepp's draft, he switches out Kiley for the equally
sonorous James Earl Jones, famed for voicing *Star Wars* villain Darth
Vader. Spielberg ultimately recruited Kiley for the film, and the actor went
on to lend his rich baritone voice to the real-life Hollywood theme park
attraction Jurassic Park: The Ride. Jones, meanwhile, was brought in to
present the behind-the-scenes documentary *The Making of Jurassic
Park*, which accompanied the film's home entertainment release.

VOICE (o.s.)
To the right, you will see a herd
of the first dinosaurs on our tour,
called Dilophosaurus.

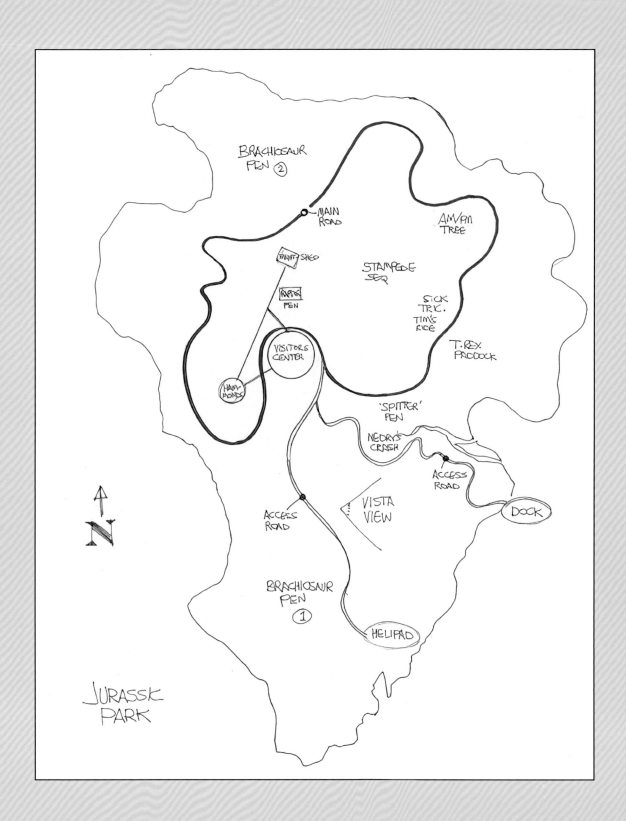

IN THE FRONT CAR,
Tim and Lex practically SLAM up
against the windows, to get a look.

> **GENNARO**
> (keeps talking)
>
> The safety. That's the problem I had
> to answer.

> **LEX**
> Shhh.

> **TIM**
> I can't see.

> **GENNARO**
> What are we looking for?

> **TIM**
> Dilophosaurus.

IN THE REAR CAR
Grant looks at his map. Ellie,
hearing the voice, reacts.

> **ELLIE**
> Oh, shit.

> **GRANT**
> Dilophosaurus.

Grant, Malcolm, and Ellie press
against the windows.

DOWN NEAR THE RIVER BANK
there are a lot of beautiful plants,
but no sign of a herd of anything.
The tour voice continues anyway.

> **VOICE (o.s.)**
> One of the earliest carnivores, we
> now know Dilophosaurus is actually
> poisonous, spitting its venom at
> its prey, causing blindness and
> eventually paralysis, allowing
> the carnivore to eat at its
> leisure. This makes Dilophosaurus a
> beautiful, but deadly addition to
> Jurassic Park.

Corny SCARY MUSIC plays over the
speaker.

IN THE FRONT CAR,

> **TIM**
> There's nothing there!

IN THE REAR CAR,

> **ELLIE**
> Alan, where?

Grant and the others sit back,
disappointed.

> **GRANT**
> Damn.

ON THE ROAD,
the cars move on. As they roll past,
we notice the headlights are on,
even in the daytime.

BELOW A Ford Explorer
steers the tour party into
Dilophosaurus territory.

OPPOSITE Concept sketch
by John Bell of Isla Nublar.
Note that it pinpoints the
place where Nedry crashes,
right next to the Spitter pen.

CUT TO:

INT CONTROL ROOM - DAY
RAY ARNOLD watches his computer
screen and the video monitors at
the same time, keeping an eye on
the cars as they move through
the park. HAMMOND hovers over his
shoulder.

ARNOLD
Vehicle headlights are on and don't
respond. Those shouldn't be running
off the car batteries.

He sighs and reaches for a clipboard
hanging next to his chair and jots
this down.

ARNOLD (cont'd)
Item one fifty-one on today's glitch
list. We've got all the problems of
a major theme park and a major zoo,
and the computer's not even on its
feet yet.

Hammond shakes his head and turns
to the TECHNICIAN to his right, who
still has his back to them, watching
a Costa Rican game show on one of his
monitors and drinking a Jolt cola.

HAMMOND
Dennis, our lives are in your hands
and you have butterfingers.

The Technician turns around his
chair and extends his arms in a
Christ-like pose. As we get a good
look at him, we get the sinking
feeling that we've seen him somewhere
before. And we have. DENNIS NEDRY is
the man who accepted a suitcase full
of cash in San Jose.

NEDRY
I am totally unappreciated in my
time. We can run the whole park from
this room, with minimal staff, for up
to three days. You think that kind
of automation is easy? Or cheap? You
know anybody who can network eight
Connection Machines and de-bug two
million lines of code for what I bid
this job? Because I'd sure as hell
like to see them try.

HAMMOND
I'm sorry about your financial
problems. I really am. But they are
your problems.

RIGHT John "Ray" Arnold
(Samuel L. Jackson), the "thin,
tense, chain-smoking," chief
engineer of Jurassic Park.

OPPOSITE TOP Dennis Nedry
(Wayne Knight) at his desk.

NEDRY
You're right, John. You're absolutely right. Everything's my problem.

HAMMOND
I will not get drawn into another financial conversation with you, Dennis. I really will not.

NEDRY
I don't think there's been any debate. There's no debate . . . my mistakes . . .

HAMMOND
I don't blame people for their mistakes, but I do ask that they pay for them.

NEDRY
Thanks, Dad.

ARNOLD
Dennis - - the headlights.

SHARK IN THE PARK

In Koepp's final draft, Nedry is watching "a Costa Rican game show" on one of his monitors. In the final film, Spielberg opted for an in-joke, inserting a clip from his own 1975 blockbuster *Jaws*, which can be seen in a small window on Nedry's monitor.

NEDRY
I'll de-bug the tour program when they get back. Okay? It'll eat a lot of computer cycles; parts of the system may go down for a while - - Don't blame me. If I am playing . . . losing memory . . .

MULDOON, who has been hovering near the video monitors as always, turns towards them, annoyed.

MULDOON
Quiet, all of you. They're coming to the tyrannosaur paddock.

SILICON DREAMS

The technology used in *Jurassic Park*'s Control Room changed over time. Crichton's novel and drafts mention Cray XMP computers and Hamachi-Hood automated sequencers, used to analyze dinosaur DNA. In Koepp's drafts, Mr. DNA references Thinking Machines as the computer of choice, and Nedry claims he's capable of networking eight "Connection Machines." First announced in 1991, the refrigerator-sized Thinking Machine Connection Machine-5 (CM-5) supercomputer was the fastest of its day. The production team managed to secure the use of several CM-5s for the film. "We actually got permission because it was something they wanted to be able to advertise [and so we] had those computers in the background—the red kind of lights, the stands," says Rick Carter.

The production also borrowed state-of-the-art computers from Silicon Graphics and Apple—worth over $1.7 million—to create the technicians' workstations. Unusually, the graphics playing on the monitors were all running in real time, rather than being fed to the display units via video playback. To achieve this, a separate computer room was built close to the Control Room set. Graphics supervisor Michael Backes managed the team responsible for cueing up the appropriate graphics from the working computers hidden away next door, using headsets to listen along as the scenes in the Control Room unfolded. Before his work on the film, Backes acted as a technical consultant on Crichton's novel. He even features in the book: A diagram representing the Jurassic Park Common User Interface lists the project supervisor as Dennis Nedry and the chief programmer as one Mike Backes. His name also appears in the film, on the cover of *Dinosaur Detectives*, a book he apparently co-authored with Alan Grant.

CUT TO:

EXT TYRANNOSAUR PADDOCK - DAY
The two Explorers drive along a high ridge and stop at the edge of the large, open plain that is separated from the road by a fifteen-foot fence, clearly marked with "DANGER!" signs and ominous-looking electrical post.

TIM, LEX, and GENNARO are pressed forward against the windows, eyes wide, waiting for you-know-who.

IN THE REAR CAR,
The voice of the radio drones on, but GRANT, ELLIE, and MALCOLM aren't even listening anymore, dying of anticipation.

> VOICE (o.s.)
> The mighty tyrannosaurus arose late in the dinosaur history. Dinosaurs ruled the earth for a hundred and fifty million years, but it wasn't until the last - -

> GRANT
> Will you turn that thing off?

Ellie flips a switch and they wait in silence - - except for Malcolm, who looks at the ceiling, thinking aloud.

> MALCOLM
> God creates dinosaurs. God destroys dinosaurs. God creates man. Man destroys God. Man creates dinosaurs.

> ELLIE
> (finishing it for him)

> Dinosaur eats man. Woman inherits the Earth.

> ARNOLD (o.s.)
> Hold on, we'll try to tempt the rex.

IN THE PADDOCK,
there is a low HUMMING sound. Out in the middle of the field, a small cage rises up into view, lifted on hydraulics from underground.

The cage bars slide down, leaving the cage's occupant standing alone in the middle of the field.

It's a goat, one leg chained to a stake. It looks around, confused, and BLEATS plaintively.

IN THE FRONT CAR,
LEX and TIM look at the goat with widely different reactions.

LEX
What's going to happen to the goat? He's going to eat the goat?!

TIM
(in heaven)
Excellent.

GENNARO
(to Lex)
What's the matter, kid, you never had lamb chops?

LEX
I happen to be a vegetarian.

GREATEST OF ALL TIME

In the novel, the tour party witness the *T. rex* devour a live goat, hearing "the sickening crunch of bones" as it's eaten. Scotch Marmo decided against including this moment, keeping the goat alive. "I used the goat offered to the *T. rex* as a means to create tension," she says. In his first draft, Koepp stoked the tension further shortly before the Main Road attack—the goat disappears before a "disembodied goat leg" lands on the sunroof of the vehicle containing Tim and Lex. The kids then watch as the *T. rex* swallows down its meal.

ABOVE The goat awaits its fate in the jaws of the *T. rex*.

OPPOSITE TOP LEFT Samuel L. Jackson as Arnold on the Control Room set. Worth over $1.7 million, the computers in the Control Room came courtesy of Silicon Graphics and Apple.

IN THE REAR CAR,

GRANT
(shakes his head)

T-rex doesn't want to be fed; he wants to hunt. You can't just suppress sixty-five million years of gut instinct.

IN THE PADDOCK
The goat waits. And waits. From the Explorers, six faces watch it expectantly. The goat tugs on its chain. It walks back and forth, nervous. It BLEATS.

IN THE REAR CAR,
Grant watches, his eyes glued, his breathing becoming a little more rapid.

IN THE FRONT CAR,
Tim and Lex can't tear their eyes away.

IN THE PADDOCK,
finally, the goat - -

- - lays down.

IN THE REAR CAR,
everyone sits back, disappointed again, as the cars pull forward to continue the tour. Malcolm picks up the microphone.

MALCOLM
Now, eventually you do plan to have dinosaurs on your dinosaur tour, right?

INT CONTROL ROOM - DAY
HAMMOND just shakes his head as Malcolm's voice comes through.

HAMMOND
I really hate that man.

OPPOSITE TOP Ian Malcolm, a figure that Koepp initially struggled with until Jeff Goldblum's casting helped the writer find the character's voice.

EXT PARK - DAY
GRANT gets into the seat, leaving MALCOLM behind ELLIE. He longingly looks out of the opposite window, while Malcolm rattles on to Ellie.

MALCOLM
You see? The tyrannosaur doesn't obey set patterns or park schedules. It's the essence of Chaos.

ELLIE
I'm still not clear on Chaos.

MALCOLM
It simply deals with unpredictability in complex systems. Its only principle is the Butterfly Effect. A butterfly can flap its wings in Peking and in Central Park you get rain instead of sunshine.

Ellie gestures with her hand to show this information has gone right over her head.

MALCOLM
I made a fly by, I go too fast.

Looking out of the opposite window, Grant sees movement at the far end of a field. He sits bolt upright, trying to get a better look.

Malcolm, looking for another example - -

MALCOLM (cont'd)
(points to the glass of water)

Here. Give me your glass of water.

He dips his hand into the glass of water. He takes Ellie's hand in his own.

MALCOLM (cont'd)
Make like hieroglyphics. Now watch
the way the drop of water falls on
your hand.

He flicks his fingers and a drop
falls on the back of Ellie's hand.

MALCOLM (cont'd)
Ready? Freeze your hand. Now I'm
going to do the same thing from the
exact same place. Which way is the
drop going to roll off?

(or)

Which way will the drop roll? Over
which finger? Or down your thumb? Or
to the other side?

ELLIE
Uh - - thumb!

(or)

The same way.

MALCOLM
It changed. Why?

(or)

Okay, back over your wrist.

(then)

Because and here is the principle of
tiny variations - - the orientations
of the hairs - -

ELLIE
Alan, listen to this.

MALCOLM
- - on your hand, the amount of
blood distending in your vessels,
imperfections in the skin - -

MALCOLM IN THE MIDDLE

Koepp's final draft made considerable efforts to add dimension to Dr. Ian Malcolm's character, "trying to find those bits of humanity," as the writer puts it. The earlier Crichton script drafts had done little to flesh out his backstory or his personality beyond what was in the novel, but as Koepp wrote, he began to get the "vibe" of the character, especially once Goldblum was locked in for the role. "I was like, 'Well, okay, I can loosen him up a little bit, I'll make them a bit of a flirt.' And then he started doing that thing that good characters do, which is surprising you." Some beats even served dual purposes, like the moment in Koepp's final draft where Malcolm tries to charm Ellie on the tour. When Malcolm puts a droplet of water on the back of her hand, he's not only showing that he's an incorrigible flirt, he's also giving a practical demonstration of chaos theory that helps audiences understand the complex ideas that underpin his particular field of study. Koepp credits Spielberg for the inspiration: "I believe the water drops on the hand was Steven's idea . . . and I wrote it up."

JOHN "RAY" ARNOLD

John "Ray" Arnold, the head engineer of Hammond's park, is described in Crichton's novel as "a thin, tense, chain-smoking man of forty-five." Although the various drafts of the screenplay brought subtle differences to the character, Crichton's characterization remained largely intact in the final film, where Arnold was played by Samuel L. Jackson. In his final draft, Koepp describes Arnold as a "chronic worrier," a trait that was less evident in Crichton's drafts, where the character is rather boastful about the park's computer systems: "It really is a hell of a system," he says. Nevertheless, he also fires a warning shot to Hammond in Crichton's first draft: "We've had to delay the Jungle River Ride because of the *Dilophosaurus*; and the Overland Ride because of the *Triceratops* charges." Although later Koepp reduced this to Arnold wryly commenting on the park's "glitch list," the writer notes there was little need to expand the character further: "He worked pretty much as he was. Given the size of the role, it would be hard to get into any kind of personal life."

>   ELLIE
>   Oh, imperfections?
>
>   MALCOLM
>   Microscopic - - never repeat, and
>   vastly affect the outcome. That's
>   what?
>
>   ELLIE
>   Unpredictability . . .
>
>   MALCOLM
>   And even if we haven't seen it yet,
>   I'm quite sure it's going on in this
>   park right now.
>
>   There's definitely something out in
>   that field, and Grant has to see it.

RIGHT Early concept art by John Bell of John "Ray" Arnold, complete with ever-present cigarette in his hand.

OPPOSITE BOTTOM Arnold (Samuel L. Jackson) realizes that Jurassic Park is offline.

>   He jerks on the door handle and
>   opens his door a few inches. He
>   looks outside towards freedom, then
>   looks around to see if anybody's
>   watching him.
>
>   Malcolm lowers his voice, becoming
>   more seductive now.

MALCOLM (cont'd)
Life's a lot like that, isn't it? You
meet someone by chance you'll never
meet again, and the course of your
whole future changes. It's dynamic -
- it's exciting - - I think.

Grant throws the door open and bolts
out of the moving car.

MALCOLM (cont'd)
There, there see?! I'm right again!

ELLIE
Alan?

MALCOLM
No one could have predicted Dr.
Grant would suddenly jump out of a
moving vehicle!

ELLIE
Alan?

She jumps out too and follows him
into the field.

MALCOLM
There's another example!

IN THE FRONT CAR,

TIM
Hey! I want to go with them!

IN THE REAR CAR,

MALCOLM
See? Here I am now, by myself,
talking to myself - -

that's Chaos Theory! What the hell am I
doing here? I'm the only one who knows
what's going on, etc., etc. . . .

INT CONTROL ROOM - DAY
HAMMOND, MULDOON, and ARNOLD stare
at the video monitor incredulously
as everyone now pours out of the cars
and follows Grant down the hill.

The cars roll on slowly, empty, their
doors hanging open.

ARNOLD
Uh - - Mr. Hammond - -

HAMMOND
Stop the program! Stop the program!

MULDOON
There you are! How many times
did I tell you we needed locking
mechanisms on the vehicle doors!

ACROSS THE ROOM
DENNIS NEDRY sneaks a peek at the
video monitor. It shows an image of
the steel door, plainly marked - -
"EMBRYONIC COLD STORAGE.
RESTRICTED!"

He looks to another monitor, which
is labeled "EAST DOCK." The monitor
shows a supply ship, moored at the
dock. Its cargo is being unloaded
and a large group of WORKERS is
filing aboard.

Nedry has something under the
counter, where no one can see it.
It's a can of shaving cream.

EXT PARK - DAY
GRANT, ELLIE, GENNARO, and the KIDS
are out in the open field, heading
towards a small stand of trees. For
the first time, we notice the sky
is darkening rather early in the
day. Tim dogs Grant's footsteps, so
excited he can hardly keep his feet
on the ground.

TIM
So like I was saying, there's this
other book by a guy named Bakker?
And he said dinosaurs died of a
bunch of diseases? He definitely
didn't say they turned into birds.

Gennaro is scared as hell, following
the others, but his head darting
left and right.

ELLIE
Alan? Where are we going? You see
something?

GENNARO
Uh - - anybody else think we
shouldn't be out here?

TIM
And his book was a lot fatter than
yours.

GRANT
Really?

ELLIE
Yours was fully
illustrated, honey.

GENNARO
Anybody at all. Feel free to speak up.

Lex stumbles and Grant takes her hand,
to stop her from falling. She looks up
at him and smiles.

Grant smiles back and tries to recover
his hand, but Lex holds tight. He's
massively uncomfortable. Ellie notices.

Suddenly they all stop in their
tracks. A huge smile spreads across
the faces of both Tim and Grant.
Grant walks forward. Tim follows.

ELLIE
Timmy, Timmy.

LEX
Come back here, blanket head.

Fearless, Tim walks forward behind
Grant.

HARDING (o.s.)
Hi everybody. Don't be scared.

Tim reaches the clearing and sees:

A Triceratops, a big one, lying on its side, blocking the light at the end of the path. It has an enormous curved shell that flanks its head, two big horns over its eyes, and a third on the end of its nose. It doesn't move, just breathes, loud and raspy, blowing up a little cloud of dust with every exhalation.

Grant stands next to Harding, almost in a daze.

                    GRANT
        Beautiful. Is it okay? Can I touch
                    it?

                    HARDING
                    Sure.

Grant walks next to the animal and strokes its head. Ellie moves forward to the animal.

ABOVE Concept art by John Bell depicts Dr. Ellie Sattler encountering a *Triceratops*.

THESE PAGES Storyboards depicting an early iteration of the scene where Sattler tends to an ailing dinosaur. In Crichton's novel and drafts, as shown here, she examines a *Stegosaurus* rather than the *Triceratops* seen in the final film.

GRANT

Oh Ellie. It's so beautiful. It's the most beautiful thing I ever saw.

ELLIE

It's my favorite.

They both kneel, checking the animal.

He furrows his brow, noticing something, all professional curiosity now. The animal's tongue, dark purple, droops limply from its mouth.

GRANT (cont'd)

Ellie, take a look at this.

ELLIE

Yeah, baby girl, it's okay.

She scratches the tongue with her fingernail. A clear liquid leaks from the broken blisters.

SICK DAY

The novel and Crichton's drafts all feature scenes in which Ellie Sattler tends to an ailing *Stegosaurus*. Scotch Marmo switched the dinosaur to a *Triceratops*. "Steven had sent me many artist renditions of potential storyboards: I was sent the *Triceratops* and used it," she states. "There is something adorable about a *Triceratops*. They are somewhere between a gentle cow and a rhino." Her script also contains a fascinating exchange between Arnold and Hammond, who admonishes the chief engineer for casually saying: "The Trike's sick." Outraged that Arnold would refer to one of his genetic miracles with a nickname, the park owner rants: "It astounds me every time what I've done here. What magic, what alchemy. We turned a piece of a rock into a dinosaur. I will never be complacent about that."

Sculpted by Stan Winston Studio team member Joey Orosco, the prone Trike was built as a fully working animatronic dinosaur. The creature was fitted with hydraulics that worked its jaw, tongue, and eye, and the belly was also rigged to move up and down, simulating the creature's troubled breathing. Spielberg was so overcome by its realism he asked Sam Neill to improvise the moment where Grant lies on the belly of the creature. "I wanted him to just breathe with it," he says. "As the *Triceratops* takes a breath, Alan Grant rises. And as the *Triceratops* exhales, Alan Grant is lowered . . . he contracts and expands with the breathing. And that really brought a tear to my eye."

"THAT'S PHARMACOLOGICAL. FROM LOCAL PLANT LIFE."

—ELLIE SATTLER

ELLIE
Micro vesicles. That's interesting.

Grant, fascinated, wanders all the way around to the back of the animal. Harding joins Ellie and hands her his penlight.

ELLIE (cont'd)
What are her symptoms?

HARDING
Imbalance, disorientation, labored breathing. Seems to happen about every six weeks or so.

ELLIE
Six weeks?

She takes the penlight from the

veterinarian and shines it in the animal's eyes.

ELLIE (cont'd)
Are there pupillary effects from the tranquilizer?

HARDING
Yes, miotic, pupils should be constricted.

ELLIE
These are dilated. Take a look.

HARDING
They are?

(checks it out)

I'll be damned.

ELLIE
That's pharmacological. From local plant life.

ABOVE The sick *Triceratops*, which was a full-sized animatronic dinosaur.

OPPOSITE Grant (Neill) examines the sick *Triceratops*.

She turns and studies the surrounding landscape. Her mind's really at work, puzzling over each piece of foliage.

                    ELLIE (cont'd)
                     (pointing)

Is that (or) this West Indian lilac?

                    HARDING
     Yes. We know they're toxic, but the
          animals don't eat them.

                    ELLIE
               Are you sure?

                    HARDING
               Pretty sure.

                    ELLIE
     There's only one way to be positive.
       I need to see some droppings.

                      (or)

        I have to see the dinosaur's
                droppings.

                    HARDING
     You won't be able to miss them.

                      (or)

DOCTOR, DOCTOR

After the film was released, Koepp "got some grief" from audience members who had read his script. "People would write letters to the studio, and they'd forward it to me. There were some complaints that, in the script, I refer to Alan Grant as 'Grant' and I refer to Ellie Sattler as 'Ellie.' He's Dr. Grant, she's Dr. Sattler." Certainly, for the scene where she tends the sick *Triceratops*, and showcases her extensive scientific knowledge, it might seem rather patronizing. "People said, 'Why does he get his last name and she gets her first? That's sexist!' And I thought, 'Not a bad point!'" While Koepp does indeed refer to the characters as 'Grant' and 'Ellie' throughout the script, he was not alone. Both Crichton, in his novel and screenplay drafts, and Scotch Marmo did exactly the same.

               Can't miss them.

Malcolm walks up to Ellie.

                    MALCOLM
               Dino droppings?

                    ELLIE
                  Yeah.

She walks away, Malcolm looks on.

ABOVE Muldoon (Bob Peck, left) takes a phone call about the incoming storm that is set to batter Isla Nublar, as Arnold (Samuel L. Jackson, center) and Hammond (Richard Attenborough) look on.

OPPOSITE TOP Dennis Nedry (Wayne Knight) puts his plan into action, stealing embryos from the cold storage facility.

INT CONTROL ROOM - DAY

HAMMOND and ARNOLD are watching the video monitors, displeased about something. Arnold is looking at one that gives them a view from the beach, looking out at the ocean. The clouds beyond are almost black with a tropical storm.

                    ARNOLD
     That storm center hasn't dissipated
     or changed course. We're going to
      have to cut the tour short, I'm
      afraid. Pick it up again tomorrow
           where we left off.

                    HAMMOND
           You're sure we have to?

                    ARNOLD
      It's not worth taking the chance,
                    John.

                    MULDOON
                 (into phone)

          Sustain winds 45 knots.

                    HAMMOND
                   (nods)

      Tell them when they get back to the
                    cars.

                    MULDOON
                 (into phone)

             Thanks, Steve.

ARNOLD
(making an announcement to the
others)

Ladies and gentlemen, last shuttle
to the dock leaves in approximately
five minutes. Drop what you are doing
and leave now.

HAMMOND
Damn!

ACROSS THE ROOM
NEDRY stares at his video monitor,
watching the boat. He's on the phone
with the MATE, whose image he can see
on the monitor. The seas around the
dock are much rougher now.

MATE
We're not well-berthed here without
a storm barrier! We may have to
leave as soon as the last of the
workers are aboard.

NEDRY
(low voice)

No, no. You stick to the plan. You
wait till they're back from the
tour.

STORM CLOUDS

An incoming storm was always a crucial part of the narrative of *Jurassic Park*, right back to Crichton's novel. In the final script draft, as thunder and rain envelop the island, the weather forces Nedry to accelerate his theft of the embryos so that he can deliver them to the boat before it departs ahead of the storm. Yet nobody on the shoot expected life to imitate art. On September 11, 1992, Kauai was hit by the devastating Hurricane Iniki. When it swept through the island, the *Jurassic* team was almost finished shooting the Hawaiian leg of the production.

The notification came early that morning, although it took time for word to spread. Set costumer Mitchell Kenney remembers arriving outside the hotel for his usual 5 a.m. pickup to find his assistant makeup supervisor Monty Westmore was already there. "Monty was always doing practical jokes," he says. "Monty goes 'Oh we're not filming today.' And I said, 'Oh stop it, Monty.' He goes, 'No, there's a hurricane coming. I think it's going to wipe out the whole island.' And I laughed at him, and I go, 'Monty, come on, where's the van at?'"

As the truth dawned on everyone, the cast and crew gathered in the hotel's ballroom to take shelter while Spielberg jumped at the opportunity to capture some footage that could be used in the film. Together with cinematographer Dean Cundey and a handful of crew members, the director ventured outside to shoot what he could. "This is when the hurricane was building and we had sustained winds of around sixty miles an hour," he says. "The breakwater was thirty feet high, and the ocean was breaking over the top of the breakwater! And we were getting shots of this occurrence." Ultimately, Spielberg and his team were able to capture some stunning storm footage that features in the completed movie.

PILE IT ON

The sizeable mound of dinosaur dung that Dr. Ellie Sattler merrily digs into as she investigates the root causes of the *Triceratops*' illness leads to one of Koepp's more memorable lines. Observing the excrement, Dr. Ian Malcolm comments: "That is one big pile of shit." The line was absent from Koepp's first draft, as was the dung itself. "Well, it's not exactly Stoppardian in its wit," says Koepp. "But that one I can safely say is mine. I enjoy vulgarity. And I enjoy an understatement!" The scene, which features a cameo from *Jurassic Park* producer Gerald R. Molen, who plays veterinarian Harding, became an iconic and much-talked-about scene. Says Dern, "For twenty years, at any restaurant I've ever been, there's a child under ten that goes up to me and says, 'Are you the lady who stuck her hand in the dinosaur poopie?' That is the question I get most commonly in my career."

ABOVE Ian Malcolm (Jeff Goldblum) pictured next to "one big pile of shit," as he so memorably terms it.

OPPOSITE Concept sketch by Mark "Crash" McCreery, showing the sick *Triceratops*.

EXT FIELD - DAY
As the weather grows darker, ELLIE, GRANT, HARDING, and MALCOLM are grouped around an enormous spoor of triceratops excreta that stands at least waist high and is covered with BUZZING flies.

              MALCOLM
    That is one big pile of shit.

Ellie has plastic gloves on that reach up to her elbows, and is just withdrawing her hand from the middle of the dung.

              ELLIE
        (to Harding)

    You're right. There's no trace of lilac berries. That's so weird, though. She shows all the classic signs of Melia toxicity.

      (thinking aloud)

    Every six weeks - -

She turns and walks out into the open field a few paces, thinking. Malcolm watches her, and looks back at the dung.

MALCOLM
(to Grant)

She's, uh - - tenacious.

GRANT
You have no idea.

MALCOLM
(to Ellie)

You will remember to wash your hands
before you eat anything?

INT CONTROL ROOM - DAY
DENNIS NEDRY is busily and
surreptitiously typing a series of
commands into his console. On his
screen, a cartoon hand winds up a
cartoon clock, moving its second hand
up to the twelve. The clock rotates
around to face us.

It has a large green dollar sign in the
middle. A big word appears on screen,
an option surrounded by forbidding red
box. "EXECUTE," it says.

EXT PARK - DAY
The skies are really foreboding
now, and there's a sense of growing
urgency. ELLIE is by the animal, a
short distance away from the group.
GRANT is near her, thinking.

GRANT
Ellie, I've been thinking there's
something about the periodicity that
doesn't add up.

ELLIE
I know.

Tim holds one of the smooth rocks up
and calls out, a little timidly.

TIM
These look kind of familiar.

GRANT
Triceratops was a constant browser,
and constant browsers would be
constantly sick.

ELLIE
Constantly sick.

GRANT
Not just every six weeks.

ELLIE
Yeah, I know.

TIM
I've seen pictures of these!

Grant turns and looks at him, a
little annoyed.

TIM
In your fully illustrated book.

Grant just rolls his eyes, but Ellie comes over and checks out the stones.

ELLIE
What's that?

A light goes on in her eyes.

ELLIE
Alan - - gizzard stones!

She throws Grant one of the stones. They look at each other in amazement.

As before, when they get excited, they talk right over each other.

GRANT
El that's it, it explains the periodicity, the - -

ELLIE
- - the undigested state of the berries because it's - -

GRANT
- - totally incidental (or)

unrelated to the feeding pattern - -

TIM
What are you guys saying?

ELLIE
(turning to Tim)

It's simple, see. Some animals like her, don't have teeth - -

GRANT
- - like birds - -

ELLIE
- - like birds. What happens is, they swallow the stones and hold them in a muscular sack in their stomachs - -

GRANT
- - a gizzard - -

ELLIE
- - which is called a gizzard, and it helps them mash their food, but what happens after a while - -

GRANT
- - what happens is that after a while, the stones get smooth, every six weeks, so the animal regurgitates them - -

ELLIE
(for Tim)

- - barfs them up - -

GRANT
- - and swallows fresh ones.

ELLIE
And when she swallows the stones, she swallows the poison berries too. That's what makes her sick.

(impressed)

Good work Tim.

She looks at Grant pointedly. Tim looks up at Grant too, smiling from ear to ear. Grant GRUNTS, not so easily convinced.

THUNDER rumbles as the storm overhead is about to bust loose. GENNARO, scared of more than one thing now, puts his foot down.

GENNARO
Doctors, if you please - - I have to insist we get moving.

ELLIE
Oh, you know, if it's alright, I'd like to stay with Dr. Harding and finish with the trike. Is that okay?

HARDING

Sure. I've got a gas powered jeep. I can drop her at the visitor's center before I make the boat with the others.

ELLIE
(to Grant)

I'll catch up with you. You can go with the others.

GRANT
Are you sure?

ELLIE
I'll just finish. Yeah, I want to finish.

There is a lightning flash now, with a tooth-rattling THUNDERCLAP right on its heels.

GENNARO
Now.

DIAGNOSING THE TRICERATOPS

In Crichton's revised draft, the inference is that the ailing dinosaur, a *Stegosaurus* in his version, is suffering from tooth decay. Scotch Marmo's take is closer to the novel, as Sattler and Grant discover the *Triceratops* has been ingesting poisonous West Indian lilac berries. In this version, Timmy helps by discovering a pile of stones, which Grant realizes are being used by the dinosaur to help digest the berries. Having Grant and Sattler lead the investigation was a way of "building confidence in Ellie and Alan's smarts," says the writer. Scotch Marmo gives further agency to Sattler later in her draft, as the paleobotanist's investigations lead her to Dr. Wu's lab where she discovers that he has been feeding the creatures growth hormones to accelerate their development. This story beat would be removed from subsequent drafts.

Grant turns and follows the others, Lex right in his tracks.

Ellie and Harding go back to the triceratops, which is starting to come back to life.

ABOVE Grant (Sam Neill) on the belly of the *Triceratops.*

ON TOUR

The tour sequence in the novel begins with the party passing the areas where small bipedal *Hypsilophodonts* should be, but there's no sign of them. As the vehicles move on, Tim spots a *Dilophosaurus* on the riverbank, then two *Triceratops*. The *pièce de résistance* comes when they watch the *T. rex* slaughter a goat. However, Crichton sensed the need to hold back on the *T. rex* in his first screenplay draft and kept it offscreen. "She's a little shy," says Ed Regis to the others. His revised draft further shuffled the deck, beginning the tour with the group's first dinosaur encounter, the *Apatosaurus*, a moment that sends Grant into spasms of delight. Scotch Marmo's draft takes a similar approach, with her tour party spotting an array of dinosaurs, including a herd of *Gallimimus* and two *Dilophosaurus*. Gradually, and with budget concerns top of mind, the production came to realize less was more. Koepp's first draft includes the sighting of one *Dilophosaurus*, "hopping, like a kangaroo." The final draft deliberately holds back on the dinosaurs in the early part of the excursion, as the group pass the *Dilophosaurus* enclosure and the *T. rex* paddock and see neither, before finally encountering the ailing dinosaur. As Hammond seethes in the final draft: "Two no-shows and one sick *Triceratops*."

As Grant reaches the Explorer, he turns back for one last look at Ellie. He raises his hand to wave, but she is turned the other way. Feeling silly, he drops his hand and goes into the woods. Just as he does, Ellie turns and waves to him, but with his back turned, he misses it too.

In this way, they say goodbye. BACK AT THE CARS, as the reflections of the GROUP approach, the first raindrops fall on the windshields of the tour vehicles. They're big, fat drops, and they kick up little clouds of dust as they SMACK into the glass.

It's going to be a hell of a storm.

EXT PARK - DUSK

It's near dark now. The wind has whipped up, and the trees are swaying.

INT CONTROL ROOM - DUSK

HAMMOND is with RAY ARNOLD, staring at the video screens.

> ARNOLD
>
> I found a way to re-route through the program. I'm turning the cars around in the rest area loop.

> HAMMOND
>
> Rotten luck, this storm. Get my grandchildren on the radio will you? I don't want them to worry about a wee bit of rain.

Arnold reaches for the hand microphone.

ACROSS THE ROOM,

DENNIS NEDRY, sweat forming on his upper lip now, is staring at his video monitor. The supply boat is still docked on the island shore, but is now being buffeted by heavy waves. Nedry whispers sharply into the phone, arguing with the MATE of the ship again, who he can see on the video monitor.

> MATE
>
> There's nothing I can do! If the Captain says we gotta go, we gotta go!

> NEDRY
>
> No, no, listen to me. You've got to give me this time. I did a test run on this thing and it took me twenty minutes. I thought I could do it in fifteen - - you've got to give me fifteen minutes.

> MATE
>
> No promises! No promises!

> NEDRY
>
> I'll be there in ten!

Arnold SNAPS a button on his console.

> ARNOLD
>
> Visitor vehicles are on their way back to the garage.

> HAMMOND
>
> So much for our first tour. Two no-shows and one sick triceratops.

> ARNOLD
>
> It could have been worse, John. It could have been a lot worse.

Dennis Nedry stands up.

He's shaking in his shoes, but trying like hell to be casual.

> NEDRY
>
> Anybody want a Coke? Anybody want something from the machines? Or a soda or something? I had too many sweets.

> (or)
>
> I thought I'd get something sweet.

Hammond and Arnold shake their heads. Nedry starts to leave, then turns back with an afterthought that is so rehearsed it's almost obvious.

> NEDRY (cont'd)
>
> Oh, I finished de-bugging the phones, but the system's compiling for eighteen minutes, or twenty. So, some minor systems may go on and off for a while. There's nothing to worry about. Simple thing . . .

> HAMMOND
>
> Okay, okay, okay, okay, that's enough! Ahh!

OPPOSITE TOP An early storyboard for a version of the tour where two *Dilophosaurus* are seen drinking from a river.

Nedry turns, stretches one finger out to his screen, and selects an option.

"EXECUTE."

At the same time, he presses the start button on his digital stopwatch he holds in his hand. A digital clock on the computer screen starts to tick down from sixty seconds, and a musical clock starts to sound too - - something like the "Jeopardy" theme.

He starts to leave - - but returns when he remembers the shaving cream can. He grabs it and leaves.

EXT PARK ROAD - NIGHT
Night has completely fallen now, and the rain has started. It's a tropical storm, the rain falling in drenching sheets on the roofs and hoods of the Explorers, which are making their way slowly back to the visitor's center.

IN THE REAR CAR,
GRANT and MALCOLM are alone. Grant is staring out the window, lost in his thoughts.

> GRANT
> You got any kids?

> MALCOLM
> Me? Oh, hell yes. Three.

> (glowing)

I love 'em. I love kids. Anything at all can and does happen.

He takes a flask from his jacket pocket and unscrews the top. His expression darkens.

> MALCOLM (cont'd)
> Same with wives, for that matter.

> GRANT
> You're married?

> MALCOLM
> Occasionally. Always on the lookout for the future ex-Mrs. Malcolm.

INT FERTILIZATION LAB - NIGHT
DENNIS NEDRY waits outside the silver door marked "EMBRYONIC COLD STORAGE," staring at the digital stopwatch in his hand.

> NEDRY
> Two - - one - -

On cue, the security lock panel goes dark and the door CLUNKS ajar.

IN THE COOLER,
Nedry hurries in and flips open the hatch on the bottom of the shaving cream can, revealing slotted compartments inside. He goes to the rack of dozens of thin glass slides. A sign says "VIABLE EMBRYOS - - HANDLE WITH EXTREME CARE!"

He takes the slides out of the rack one by one. They're labeled

- - "STEGOSAURUS," "APATOSAURUS," "TYRANNOSAURUS REX" - - and puts them into the can.

INT CONTROL ROOM - NIGHT
ARNOLD is staring at his terminal, puzzled. On the screen, glowing red and blue lines are blinking off, in succession.

> ARNOLD
> What?

HAMMOND comes up behind him, as does ROBERT MULDOON.

> HAMMOND
> What?

ARNOLD

The door security systems are
shutting down.

HAMMOND

Well, Nedry said a few systems would
go off-line, didn't he?

INT REAR CAR - NIGHT
GRANT and MALCOLM still wait in
their car. They don't notice, but
the video screen in the middle of
their front console suddenly goes
black.

Malcolm continues their conversation.

EX-MRS. MALCOLM

The conversation between Grant and Malcolm in Koepp's final draft,
where the chaos theorist reveals he's got three kids and says
he's "always on the lookout for the future ex–Mrs. Malcolm" would
seem to be tailor-made for the character. In fact, Koepp's first draft,
which excluded Malcolm, sees the line spoken by another character,
Gennaro. "I'm always on the lookout for an ex–Mrs. Gennaro," says
the lawyer, while also revealing to Grant that he's been married
three times. He then inquires about Dr. Sattler, before asking if she
and Grant are together. "No. Yes," replies Grant. "I don't know. I'm
not exactly experienced in these matters." Although this line didn't
make it to the final screenplay, it further showcases the ambiguity
of the Grant/Sattler union that Koepp weaved into his drafts.

> access security
access: PERMISSION DENIED.
> access security grid
access: PERMISSION DENIED.
> access main security grid
access: PERMISSION DENIED....and...
YOU DIDN'T SAY THE MAGIC WORD!
YOU DIDN'T SAY THE MAGIC WORD!
YOU DIDN'T SAY THE MAGIC WORD!
YOU DIDN'T SAY THE MAGIC WORD!
YOU DIDN'T SAY THE MAGIC WORD!
YOU DIDN'T SAY THE MAGIC WORD!
YOU DIDN'T SAY THE MAGIC WORD!

ABOVE Nedry's digital trap is sprung as the Jurassic Park computer systems go into lockdown.

OPPOSITE BOTTOM Arnold (Samuel L. Jackson) is confounded by Nedry's "hacker crap."

                    MALCOLM
        By the way, Dr. Sattler – she's not
          like, uh, available, is she? – –

                     GRANT
                     Why?

                    MALCOLM
          Why? Oh, I'm sorry. Are you two,
          uh – – are? I wish you the best
                     luck.

        The cars jerk to a stop. The lights
        in the vehicles and along the road go
        out, plunging them into blackness.
        Grant jerks his hands away from
        the steering column, immediately
        assuming it's his fault.

                     GRANT
                What'd I touch?!

                    MALCOLM
               You haven't touched

                     (or)

          didn't touch anything. We're
                stopping. (or)

               We've stopped.

                     GRANT
          I must've touched something. This
          happens all the time. It must be my
            fault. Machines hate me.

                    MALCOLM
             Machines hate you?

                     GRANT
            Yeah, they hate me.

                    MALCOLM
          You want to talk about this?

                     GRANT
                     No.

EXT JURASSIC PARK – NIGHT
Nedry's jeep SPLASHES up to the
giant gates that lead into Jurassic
Park. NEDRY jumps out and hurries to
the control panel on the side of the
cement supports.

He FLICKS a switch and the gates
CLICK unlocked.

He jumps back in the car and noses
into the gates, shoving them open
far enough to drive through.

He ROARS into the park grounds.

EXT CONTROL ROOM – NIGHT
RAY ARNOLD stares at his terminal,
aghast, as row upon row of colored
lights crawls off on his screen.

                    ARNOLD
          Woah, woah, woah, what the hell,
                what the hell?

                    HAMMOND
                  What now?

                    ARNOLD
          Fences are failing, all over the
          park! A few minor systems, he said!

HAMMOND
(to MULDOON, pissed)

Find Nedry! Check the vending machines!

ARNOLD
The monitors are failing.

Muldoon heads for the door just as all the video monitors in the control room go out with a faint electronic ZIP.

The three of them freeze for a moment, looking at each other. The tension in the room goes up a notch.

HAMMOND
(to Arnold)

Use Nedry's terminal. Get it all back on. He can de-bug later.

Arnold pushes off on the floor and whizzes over to Nedry's

master terminal in his chair. With one stroke of his arm, he brushes all the loose junk off Nedry's station -- junk food, soda cans, torn out magazine pages - - and tries to work.

ARNOLD
God, look at this workstation.

The "Jeopardy"-type music is playing a little faster now. Muldoon steps forward, growing alarmed.

MULDOON
The raptor fences aren't out, are they?

ARNOLD
(checks)

No, they're still on.

HAMMOND
Why the hell would he turn the others off?!

EXT PARK ROAD - NIGHT

A wire mesh fence in front of us
has a very clear sign: DANGER!
ELECTRIFIED FENCE!
This Door Cannot Be Opened When
Fence is Armed!

A hand reaches out, grabs the fence
by the bare wire, flips a latch, and
shoves the door open. No sparks fly.

DENNIS NEDRY runs from the fence back
to his jeep, drops it in gear, and
tears off down the park road. The
rain is absolutely flowing down now,
the road is rapidly turning to mud.

IN THE JEEP,
Nedry can barely see through the
windshield. He's driving as fast as
possible, checking his watch every
few seconds.
He leans forward, squinting to see
through the windshield, wiping off
the condensation with his free hand.
A fork in the road rushes into view.
He jumps on the brakes - - too late.
The jeep careens into a signpost.

NEDRY
Shit!

He throws the door open and hurries
to the fallen sign: "To The Docks."
He props it up - the directional
arrow swings hopelessly on a nail.
He clenches his jaws and growls.

Soaked, Nedry stomps back to his car.

Although he doesn't look too convinced, he drops the car in gear and speeds off to the left.

EXT CONTROL ROOM - NIGHT
HAMMOND still hovers over ARNOLD's shoulder while he works at Nedry's terminal. Arnold MUTTERS to himself as he tries another command.

> ARNOLD
> - - access main program grid - -

He punches a button, but a BUZZER sounds and a little cartoon image of Nedry appears on the screen and waves its little finger disapprovingly.

> CARTOON NEDRY
> "You didn't say the magic word!"

> ARNOLD
> (livid)
> Please, God damn it! I hate this hacker crap!

He SMACKS the top of the monitor, furious. The game show music plays still faster.

> HAMMOND
> Call Nedry's people in Cambridge!

Arnold whisks across the floor in his chair and snatches up the nearest phone. He punches for an outside line.

> ARNOLD
> Phones are out too.

> HAMMOND
> Where did the vehicles stop?

EXT TYRANNOSAUR PADDOCK - NIGHT
BAAA! The goat that was brought up from underground earlier is still tethered in the same place, BLEATING in the pouring rain.

The two Explorers sit still in the middle of the road. A man's form races back from the front car to the rear car.

IN THE REAR CAR,
GRANT, soaking wet, gets back into the car and closes the door behind him. MALCOLM turns to him.

> GRANT
> Their radio's out too. Gennaro said to stay put.

> MALCOLM
> The kids okay?

> GRANT
> Well, I didn't ask. Why wouldn't they be?

> MALCOLM
> Kids get scared.

> GRANT
> What's to be scared about? It's just a little hiccup in the power.

> MALCOLM
> I didn't say I was scared.

> GRANT
> I didn't say you were scared.

> MALCOLM
> I know.

> GRANT
> Fine.

Malcolm turns and looks out at the driving rain, and the fence that stands between them and the tyrannosaur paddock. He is scared.

OPPOSITE Concept art by John Bell shows the tour vehicle at the *T. rex* paddock.

IN THE FRONT CAR,
GENNARO, LEX, and TIM wait, bored. The rain drums on the roof monotonously. Tim is upside down in the front seat. Lex pushes his legs up, and he swings them down.

> TIM
>
> Up and down, up and down!

> GENNARO
> (sotto)
>
> I can't believe we invited Ian Malcolm.

> TIM
>
> People were gettin' bloody noses - - things on your head - - aneurisms - -

> LEX
> (a little dreamy)
>
> I think Dr. Grant is really - - smart.

> GENNARO
>
> Now he'll write a bunch of (letters) papers, go on Larry King Live, say we're irresponsible - -

Tim climbs into the back seat. Lex hits him with her hat as he moves by her.

> LEX
>
> Don't scare me.

- - - - - - - - - - - - - - - - - - - -

Tim finds something under the seat and sits up abruptly, holding what looks like a heavy-duty pair of safety goggles.

> GENNARO
>
> Hey! Where did you find those things?

NIGHT VISIONS

The night-vision goggles first appear in Crichton's novel, given to Tim by Ed Regis to keep the boy entertained during the tour. Tim soon uses them to spot the *T. rex*'s arrival, the creature's eyes glowing "bright green" in the gloom. Alerting Grant, Lex uses binoculars—presumably the same equipment, though never specified—to spot juvenile raptors climbing aboard the supply ship, the *Anne B*, before it sails away to the Costa Rican mainland.

In Crichton's first draft, Tim uses the goggles to see Nedry handing over stolen embryos to the boat captain. In the author's revised draft, at Lex's urging, Tim also spies raptors climbing aboard the ship. Scotch Marmo retained the idea, with Tim and Lex using the goggles to spy on Nedry as he delivers a portable incubator containing stolen eggs to the *Anne B*. While Koepp ditched the idea that Tim and Lex would witness Nedry's foul deeds, he retained the night-vision goggles.

In the final draft, Gennaro tells Tim off when the boy finds them in a box under his seat. "Are they heavy?" he asks. "Then they're expensive. Put them back." Ignoring Gennaro, Tim uses them to spot the *T. rex* in the dark. Art director John Bell was tasked with designing the goggles prop for filming. "I just started coming up with different shapes that I thought were pretty cool-looking and interesting," says Bell. "I did maybe a couple of versions before they landed on the one that ended up in the movie. The only thing that Steven said was scale them up bigger. So they're very big on the kid's face when he puts them on."

ABOVE An early storyboard panel shows Ed Regis placating Tim with the night-vision goggles.

OPPOSITE PAGE With night-vision goggles in hand, Tim Murphy (Joseph Mazzello) realizes that something big is coming their way.

ABOVE A set of six concept drawings by John Bell showing the escape of the *T. rex* from its paddock, as seen through the lenses of Tim's night-vision goggles.

OPPOSITE Concept art by John Bell showing Tim wearing the distinctive yellow and green night-vision goggles.

>   TIM
>   In a box under my seat.
>
>   GENNARO
>   Are they heavy?
>
>   TIM
>   Yeah.
>
>   GENNARO
>   Then they're expensive. Put them back.

He leans back and closes his eyes. Tim ignores him and puts on the goggles.

- - - - - - - - - - - - - - - - - -

Tim stares out the back window of the Explorer with Grant and Malcolm in it, behind them. The image is bright fluorescent green.

RIPPLE EFFECT

The introduction of the *T. rex* went through a number of iterations. Crichton's revised draft, for example, sees "a claw grip the fence," as thunder crashes and a terrified Ed Regis realizes the power is out. The Scotch Marmo draft makes good use of the lightning, as flashes reveal the creature suddenly standing on the Main Road. But it was Spielberg's flash of genius that truly elevated the scene. In Koepp's drafts, the script calls for the approaching footsteps of the *T. rex*: "BOOM. BOOM. BOOM." A cup of water on the dashboard begins to ripple, an idea the director had envisioned during a journey to work one day when a loud car stereo caused reverberations in his vehicle. It's an ominous moment, accentuated by the work of Gary Rydstrom, who created *Jurassic Park*'s creature sounds. Rydstrom used sonic booms to replicate the initial, faraway sound of the *T. rex*'s footsteps, and then as it nears, Rydstrom deployed the sound of redwood trees being chopped down to give the sense the dinosaur was crashing through the foliage. "We didn't even know if the computers [programmed by ILM] would actually make the dinosaurs credible at that point," recalls Rick Carter. "They were doing tests when Steven came up with that kind of boom, boom. And I remember laughing with him saying, 'Boy, you are really upping the ante here as to what you better deliver!' He said, 'I know! I just hope *they* can deliver!'"

THESE PAGES Storyboards depict the tense moments that signal the start of the Main Road *T. rex* attack.

>   TIM
>   Oh, cool! Night vision!

As Tim watches, the door of the rear Explorer opens, and a hand reaches out, holding an empty canteen out to catch some rain water.

IN THE REAR CAR
Grant pulls the canteen back in, closes the door, and takes a drink. He and Malcolm wait.

IN THE FRONT CAR
Tim continues to stare out of the back window with the goggles. He swings his legs - - but suddenly stops. He feels something. He pulls off the goggles and turns back. He moves into the back seat with Lex who is tapping her hat, and reaches forward to still her hand.

BOOM. BOOM. BOOM.

>   TIM
>   Did you feel that?
>
>   (or)
>
>   Can you feel that?

She doesn't answer.

Tim leans over to the front passenger seat and looks at the two

plastic cups of water that sit in
the recessed holes on the dashboard.
As he watches, the water in the
glasses vibrates, making concentric
circles - -

- - then it stops - -

- - and then it vibrates again.
Rhythmically. Like from footsteps.

BOOM. BOOM. BOOM.

> GENNARO
> (not entirely convinced)

What is that? M-Maybe it's the power
    trying to come back on.

Tim jumps into the back seat and
puts the goggles on again.

> LEX
> What is that?

> GENNARO
> What is what?

Tim turns and looks out the side
window. He can see the area where
the goat is tethered. Or was
tethered. The chain is still there,
but the goat is gone.

BANG!

They all jump, and Lex SCREAMS
as something hits the Plexiglas
sunroof of the Explorer, hard. They
look up.

It's a bloody, disembodied goat leg.

> GENNARO
> Oh, Jesus. Jesus.

Tim whips around to look out the side
window again. His mouth pops open,
but no sound comes out. Through the
goggles, he sees an animal claw, a

huge one, gripping the cables of the
"electrified" fence.

Tim whips the goggles off and presses
forward, against the window. He looks
up, up, then cranes his head back
further, to look out the sunroof.
Past the goat's leg, he can see - -

- - Tyrannosaurus rex. It stands
maybe twenty-five feet high, forty
feet long from nose to tail, with
an enormous, boxlike head that must
be five feet long by itself. The
remains of the goat hang out of the
rex's mouth. It tilts its head back
and swallows the animal in one big
gulp.

ON THE ROAD,
Gennaro runs away, as fast as he can, right past the second car, towards a cement block outhouse twenty or thirty yards away.

He reaches it, ducks inside, and pulls the door after him -- but there's no latch, just a round hole in the unfinished door. Gennaro backs into a stall, frantic. The whole bathroom begins to shake.

IN THE REAR CAR,
Grant and Malcolm turn in the direction Gennaro went.

Gennaro can't even speak. His hand claws for the door handle, he shoulders it open, and takes off, out of the car.

GRANT
Where does he think he's going?

LEX
(freaking out)

MALCOLM
When you gotta go, you gotta go.

He left us! He left us alone! Dr. Grant! Dr. Grant! He left us! He left us!

Malcolm looks the other way, out the passenger window. As he watches, the fence begins to buckle, its posts

collapsing into themselves, the
wires SNAPPING free.

MALCOLM
What was that all about? - -

Grant now turns and watches as,
ahead of them, the "DANGER!" sign
SMACKS down on the hood of the first
Explorer. The entire fence is coming
down, the posts collapsing, the
cables SNAPPING as - -

- - the T-rex chews its way through
the barrier.

They watch in horror as the T-rex
steps over the ruined barrier and
into the middle of the park road.
It just stands there for a moment,
swinging its head from one vehicle
to the other.

IN THE FRONT CAR,
The rex strides around to the side
of the car and peers down, from high
above. Tim leaps into the front
seat and pulls the driver's door
shut. Both kids are terrified,
breathing hard, unable to speak.

OPPOSITE TOP A storyboard
shows Gennaro bolting from
the tour vehicle in fear.

OPPOSITE BOTTOM "When
you gotta go": Malcolm (Jeff
Goldblum, *left*) and Grant
(Sam Neill) watch as Gennaro
flees the Ford Explorer.

ABOVE The *T. rex*
swallows down the goat.

The T-rex turns and strides quickly
back towards them. It circles,
slowly, bending over to look in at
them through the window.

Grant and Malcolm sit trembling in
the front seat, watching as the giant
legs stride past their windows.

> GRANT
> (a quivery whisper)

> Keep absolutely still - - its
> vision's based on movement!

> MALCOLM
> You're sure?!

> GRANT
> (pause)

> Relatively.

Malcolm freezes as the rex bends down
and peers right in through his window.
The dinosaur's giant, yellowing eye is
only slightly smaller than the entire
pane of glass.

> TIM
> Please! Please!

IN THE REAR CAR,

> MALCOLM
> Boy, do I hate being right all the
> time.

> GRANT
> Look at that!

ABOVE A storyboard depicts
the moment the *T. rex*'s foot
squelches into Main Road mud
next to a stalled tour vehicle.

RIGHT The *T. rex* breaks out
of the paddock and stomps
out into the road between
the two tour vehicles.

OPPOSITE TOP Lex (Ariana
Richards) uses a flashlight
to get a better look at
the attacking *T. rex*.

The T-rex pulls away slightly, then reaches down and BUMPS the car with its snout, rocking it.

IN THE FRONT CAR,
Lex is rummaging around in the back cargo area, looking for something, anything. She finds a flashlight.

ON THE ROAD,
The front car lights up from within as Lex switches on the flashlight.

The dinosaur raises its head. It turns slowly from the second car to the first car, drawn by the light. Making a decision, it strides over to the first vehicle. FAST.

MAIN ROAD MOMENTS

In conjunction with Spielberg and his creative team, Scotch Marmo was instrumental in developing the Main Road attack. The idea of Lex finding a flashlight, which then inadvertently attracts the *T. rex*, first appeared in her draft, as did the moment in which Grant uses a flare to distract the predator as it begins to tear apart the vehicle containing Lex and Tim. Her draft also added the moment when Grant and Lex grab onto a broken fence cable, swinging over the side of the embankment and using it to avoid the vehicle, with Tim still in it, as it's pushed over the edge by the *T. rex*. With Lex tightly grabbing Grant's neck, the writer suggests the scene had deeper layers of meaning: "The choking of Grant as they swing on the cable is a metaphor for Grant's feelings of being suffocated by children."

"TURN IT OFF, LEX! TURN IT OFF!"

—TIM MURPHY

ABOVE The *T. rex* uses its snout to nudge a tour vehicle before going in for a more aggressive attack.

OPPOSITE BOTTOM Storyboard panel depicts an overhead shot of the fearsome *T. rex* as it bears down on Tim and Lex in their tour vehicle.

IN THE FRONT CAR,
Tim and Lex can only stare out of the windows as the T-rex reaches their car and starts to circle it.

The rex bends down and looks in through the front windshield, then the side window. Tim is eye to eye with the thing for a second, then the dinosaur raises its head up, above the car.

> LEX
> I'm sorry - - I'm sorry - -

> TIM
> Turn it off, Lex! Turn it off!

Tim climbs over the seat and joins Lex.

> TIM (cont'd)
> Where is the button then?

> LEX
> I don't know, I don't know. I'm sorry - -

TIM
Why did you do this?

LEX
I don't know! I'm sorry!

The Kids look up, through the sunroof, as the head goes higher, and higher, and higher, and then the rex turns, looks straight down at them through the sunroof, opens its mouth wide and - -

- - ROARS.

The windows RATTLE, Lex SCREAMS, the flashlight goes on again, and the tyrannosaur strikes.

SMASH! The thing's head hits the plastic sunroof, knocking the whole frame right out of the roof of the car and down into the vehicle. The bubble falls down onto Tim and Lex, trapping them, and the animal lunges down, through the hole, SNAPPING at them.

52C

CRANE-up ends...

MAIN ROAD-
NIGHT-
RAIN

MR-9

Tim, whose feet were caught above him, pushes back, only an inch of glass between him and the dinosaur's teeth.

IN THE REAR CAR,
Grant and Malcolm watch in horror as the dinosaur claws at the side of the vehicle with one of its powerful hind legs.

It pushes, starting to tip the car over.

> MALCOLM
> Oh my God!

> GRANT
> We gotta do something.

> MALCOLM
> What? What can we do?

> GRANT
> There's gotta be something - -

The Plexiglas holds, though and protects Tim and Lex even as it pins them to the seats. The T-rex continues to push down, and the glass GROANS, crack lines racing across it.

Grant looks around, climbs over the seat. He tears apart the back area, searching - and finally finds a metal case. He opens it, finding flares. He grabs one and moves quickly back to the driver's seat and opens the door. Malcolm grabs a flare, too.

IN THE FRONT CAR,
the glass windows SHATTER, the Kids are thrown to the side, and the Explorer tilts.

The rex bends down and nudges the car with its head, rolling it up on its side. Tim and Lex tumble around.

ON THE ROAD
the T-rex starts to nudge the Explorer toward the barrier. Over the barrier, there is a gentle terraced area at one side where the rex emerged from, but the car isn't next to that, it's next to a sharp precipice, representing a fifty or sixty foot drop.

The car, upside down now, is pushed near the edge.

The rex towers over the car. Like a dog, it puts one foot on the chassis and tears at the undercarriage with its jaws.

CLOSE TO THE EDGE

David Koepp was never entirely convinced by the scene in which the *T. rex* pushes the tour car over the barrier at the edge of the road. His final draft reads: "Over the barrier, there is a gentle terraced area at one side where the rex emerged from, but the car isn't next to that, it's next to a sharp precipice, representing a fifty or sixty foot drop." Onscreen, it's clear that the road is hemmed in by jungle on either side. "Then the *T. rex* attacks, and the car starts to spin around . . . and they're shoved to the edge of what is now a perilous cliff. That has never been there before," says Koepp. During the shoot, the screenwriter questioned Spielberg about this geographical trick. "I said, 'Aren't we going to wonder where the cliff came from?'" Spielberg pointed to the life-size Stan Winston–created animatronic dinosaur. "And he said, 'There's a *T. rex* right there!'" In other words, the director knew that audiences would be too enraptured by this terrifying creature to notice the sudden appearance of a sheer drop.

Biting at anything it can get a hold of, it rips the rear axle free, tosses it aside, and bites into a tire.

The tire EXPLODES, startling the animal.

INSIDE THE CAR,
Tim and Lex are trapped inside the rapidly flattening car. As the frame continues to buckle, they crawl toward the open rear window, the car collapsing behind them. Mud and rain water pour into what little space there is left.

THESE PAGES Storyboards break down the key moments in the *T. rex*'s attack, as it rolls the tour vehicle over and sends the kids tumbling.

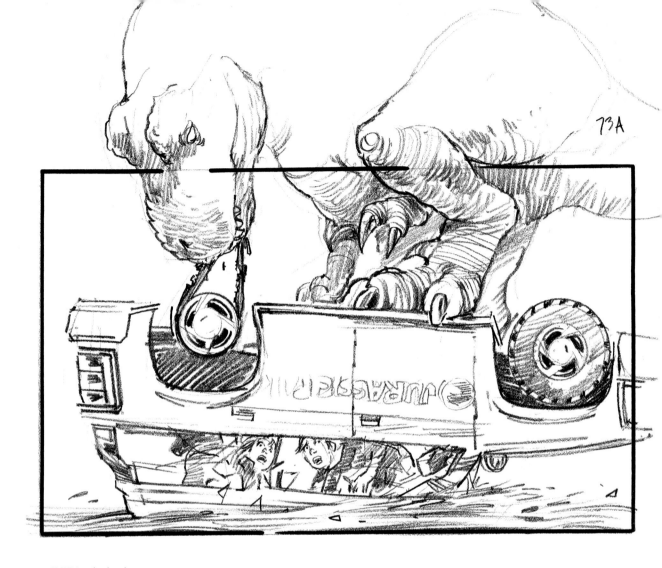

73A

ABOVE A storyboard panel shows the *T. rex* attacking the tour vehicle, with Tim and Lex trapped inside.

OPPOSITE TOP Grant (Sam Neill) lights a flare to distract the *T. rex* during the Main Road attack.

OPPOSITE BOTTOM A storyboard panel depicting the moment Grant tries to lure the *T. rex* away from Tim and Lex's vehicle.

Tim is ahead, nearing the back window, when there is a CRUNCH and a seat comes down, pinning him.

ON THE ROAD,
the dinosaur backs up, dragging the Explorer, swinging it left and right. It seems ready to fling it over the edge.

Grant gets out of his car. He's holding the flare in one hand, which he pulls the top off of. Bright flames shoot out the end of it.

GRANT
Hey! Hey! Over here!

The T-rex turns and looks at him.

Grant waves the flare slowly in front of him from side to side.

The T-rex follows his moving arm, eyes locked on the flare. Grant looks over to the wall, and tosses the flare over the edge of the barrier. The rex lunges after it - -

Unclear with Grant's plan, Malcolm
leaps out of the car and tries to
scare up the T-rex's attention with
his own newly lit flare. He begins to
wave it at the animal. Grant sees
him - -

                    GRANT
    Ian! Freeze! Freeze! Get rid of the
                    flare!

                   MALCOLM
                 Get the kids!

Malcolm inches back slowly, then   The T-rex sees the movement. It whirls
takes off, running for his life down   and takes off after Malcolm, fast.
the road. He runs to the cement
block outhouse Gennaro went into   Malcolm runs as fast as he can,
earlier.   approaching the outside just steps
                                        ahead of the T-rex.

"GET THE KIDS!"
—IAN MALCOLM

ABOVE Malcolm (Jeff Goldblum) follows Grant's lead and lights a flare to lead the *T. rex* away from the kids.

OPPOSITE Storyboard panels showing Gennaro being eaten by the *T. rex* while trying to hide from the dinosaur in a bathroom.

But not far enough ahead. Without even slowing down, the rex leans forward and flicks Malcolm into the air with its snout.

It's just a nudge for the rex, but it sends Malcolm sailing right through a wooden portion of the wall, and into the building.

IN THE RESTROOM
Gennaro, who cowers in a corner, SCREAMS as the head of the T-rex EXPLODES through the front of the building, sending chunks of cement flying in all directions inside. The roof collapses; Gennaro tries to protect himself from the falling junk.

ON THE ROAD
Grant gets on his feet and watches as the T-rex noses around in the rubble.

It seems to find something. It lunges, and Grant can hear Gennaro SCREAMING, the sound piercing - -

- - until it abruptly stops.

Grant scrambles over to the car.

> GRANT
> Tim! Lex!

> LEX
> Dr. Grant! Dr. Grant!

He lays on the ground, looking inside, and sees Lex staring up at him, conscious, her face covered in mud.

> GRANT
> Are you okay? Can you move?

> (calling into the car)

> Tim! Are you okay?

- - - - - - - VERSION 1 - - - - - - -

> GRANT
> Tim, are you okay?

> TIM
> I'm stuck. The seat's got my feet!

> GRANT
> Tim, I'll come back for you. I'll get Lex out first.

ED'S DEAD

Throughout the various iterations of the *T. rex* attack, Ed Regis was always the victim. The novel sees the terrified publicist soil his pants in fear, then abandon Tim and Lex as he flees their vehicle. After hiding between some boulders, where he is attacked by leeches, he's then torn apart by a juvenile *T. rex*, a killing observed from afar by Grant. Crichton's first draft dropped the juvenile *T. rex* but saw Regis killed by the adult dinosaur in a nearby forest. The revised draft simplified matters as the adult *T. rex* chases Regis down the road when he makes a dash for it, slaughtering him off camera.

Scotch Marmo also cut the juvenile *T. rex* in favor of the adult but kept the sequence of events close to that in the novel, even including the leeches and Grant witnessing Regis's death from afar. It was only when Koepp came on board that the scene changed. His first draft sees Regis cower in a toilet block before the *T. rex* smashes its way in, savaging the PR manager to death, while Gennaro is butted out of the way. But as Koepp's draft developed, Dr. Ian Malcolm was restored and Regis was dropped, which altered the sequence. "Cutting Ed Regis was a breakthrough on that script," says Koepp. "Malcolm was going to take up a lot of real estate. You have limited screen time to give to your characters. So if he came in, somebody had to go."

With Regis out, it was Gennaro who ran to the toilet in terror. According to Rick Carter, the idea that it would be the lawyer who met his fate on the can came from Spielberg. Meeting with the director to discuss a shot Spielberg wanted to capture in which Grant would be framed next to the enormous *T. rex* head, their conversation was interrupted by a business call that the director needed to take. "Steven comes back, and he goes, 'I got it!' I go, 'What?' He says, 'Well, it's not Grant. It's the lawyer.' He knew the audience would accept that the lawyer gets eaten. They wouldn't accept that Grant was gonna get damaged."

READING BETWEEN THE LINES

In his final draft, Koepp included some dialogue variations—additional lines that gave Spielberg and the actors extra options during the shoot. "Steven didn't necessarily film them all," the writer clarifies. "I think there were just a lot of ideas. And he wanted to have options. And there was a wealth of good material." For instance, in the scene where Grant tries to free the kids from the crushed tour car, Koepp supplied two possible versions. In one, which appears in the finished film, Tim can't wriggle free. In the other, not used in the film, Lex screams that Tim has been knocked out before she yells "Daddy, daddy!" out of sheer fear.

ABOVE Grant (Sam Neill, left) and Lex (Ariana Richards) stay still and quiet as the mighty *T. rex* makes its presence felt.

OPPOSITE Storyboards show Grant rescuing Lex from the half-crushed tour vehicle.

```
- - - - - - - VERSION 2 - - - - - -


              LEX
He's knocked out! He's knocked out!
Dr. Grant! Dr. Grant! Daddy, daddy!

             GRANT
      Let's get you out.
```

```
- - - - - - - - - - - - - - - -

Grant reaches in and drags her out.

         GRANT (cont'd)
     Are you okay? Good girl.

Grant tries to find Tim.

         GRANT (cont'd)
           Tim? Tim?

Lex, staring over his shoulder,
SCREAMS. Grant whirls, covering her
mouth at the same time.

         GRANT (cont'd)
  Shhh! Don't move! It can't see us if
         we don't move.

Lex looks at him like he's crazy,
but freezes. They wait. BOOM! A big
T-rex footprint smacks down in front
of them as the dinosaur approaches
the car again. It leans down, right
```

past them, and SNIFFS the car, ragged bits of flesh and clothing hanging from its teeth.

Not finding anything, the dinosaur swings its head away, SNORTING loudly through its nose. Grant's hat flies off his head. Still, he doesn't move.

The rex walks to the back of the car. It bends down.

WHAP! The car spins as it is pushed from behind by the rex.

Grant and Lex are pushed in front of it, helpless. They scramble around on their knees, trying to keep ahead of the car, which the rex is now pushing even closer to the edge of the barrier.

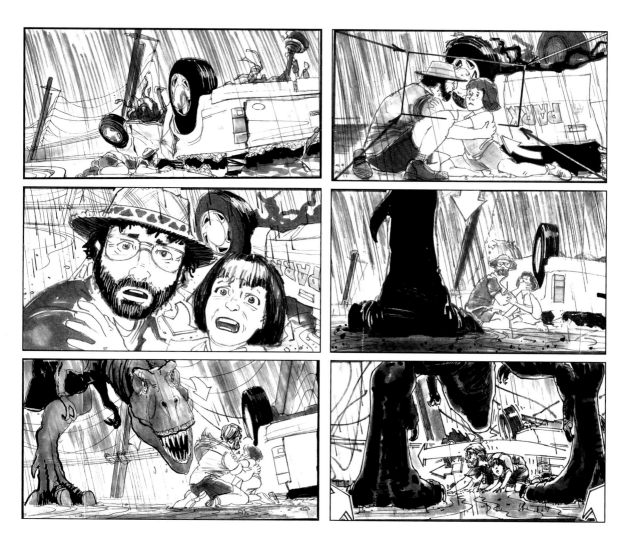

Grant and Lex crawl quickly, but the car is moving faster, catching up to them.

INSIDE THE CAR
Tim awakens and SCREAMS. He tries to untangle himself.

ON THE ROAD,
the T-rex looms over Lex and Grant, who are trapped between the car and the sixty foot drop.

INSIDE THE CAR,
the rex bends down and sees Tim. Tim backs away, furiously, but there's almost no room to move in there. The rex opens its mouth wide and stretches its tongue into the car.

Tim screams and kicks as the tongue tries to wrap around him. But it fails, and withdraws from the car.

ON THE ROAD,
the T-rex still tries to get to Grant and Lex, pushing the car, spinning on its roof. Grant and Lex scramble, trying to avoid being caught by the T-rex and crushed by the car.

> GRANT
> This way!

The back of the car almost crushes them against the barrier - -

> GRANT (cont'd)
> Get back!

They move, as the rex continues to move the car towards the edge. Grant finally gets on the wall, Lex follows.

The T-rex ROARS in frustration. It bends down for one final lunge at the car.

Grant sees it coming. He grabs one of the dangling fence cables on the other side of the barrier.

> GRANT (cont'd)
> Grab a hold of me!

She wraps her arm around his neck. He scrambles to the edge of the barrier, and starts to climb down.

> LEX
> (screaming)
>
> Timmy! Timmy!

The cable is slick with rain, and it's all Grant can do to hang on as he and Lex slide rapidly down. Above them, the vehicle is now teetering

over the edge, threatening to drop right on top of them if they didn't hurry.

Grant GASPS, as Lex has unwittingly started to choke him as she holds on for dear life.

> GRANT
>
> You're choking me!

The car GROANS, nearly over the edge now. Grant looks to the side. There are other cables, out of the line of the car's impending drop. His feet scrambling along the concrete wall, Grant tries to swing over towards one.

> GRANT (cont'd)
>
> Grab a wire!

But he falls short. His momentum carries them back the other way, but on the second swing Lex manages to grab hold of the second cable.

> LEX
>
> I got it!

ABOVE Early concept art of the Main Road *T. rex* attack by Craig Mullins.

The car falls. Lex and Grant are clear by inches, clinging to the second cable.

LEX
Timmy!

The car CRUNCHES into the leafy top of a tree, resting on its roof some fifteen feet below them.

The T-rex stares down at them, but they are safely out of its reach.

It ROARS once more, in a final fit of frustration, and turns - -

INT   CONTROL ROOM   NIGHT
JOHN HAMMOND is livid.

HAMMOND
I will kill Nedry. I will kill him.

MULDOON bursts through the door.

HAMMOND
(to Muldoon)

Well?

MULDOON
There's no sign of him anywhere.

The game show music is louder and faster now, very annoying.

HAMMOND
Ray will you please switch off

(or)

stop that music?!

RAY ARNOLD's cigarette is practically burning his lips, down to almost nothing in his mouth. He hovers over NEDRY's computer terminal, which is a mass of incomprehensible commands that scroll by quickly as he futilely examines each one of them.

Muldoon paces. ELLIE stares at Arnold in amazement.

ELLIE
Are we getting anywhere with these procedures of yours? I mean, what's hanging us up?

ARNOLD
I ran a key check on every stroke Nedry entered today. It's all pretty standard stuff, until this one - -

ELLIE
(stands, joins the group at the computer)

What one?

THESE PAGES Storyboards show the moment in which the tour vehicle is pushed over a precipice by the *T. rex*, leaving Grant and Lex hanging precariously on a cable.

He points to his computer screen, to a specific series of commands. The others crowd over his shoulder and stare at the screen.

ARNOLD
"Keycheck /space -o keycheck off safety -o." He's turning the safety systems off. He doesn't want anybody to see what he's about to do. Now look at this next entry, it's the kicker. "Wht.rbt.obj." Whatever it did, it did it all. But with Keycheck off, the computer didn't file the keystrokes. Only way to find them now is to search the computer's lines of code one by one.

ELLIE
How many lines of code are there?

ARNOLD
Uh - - about two million.

ELLIE
Two million - - great. That would help.

(or)

Oh good, that'll take no time.

HAMMOND
Robert - - I wonder if perhaps you would be kind

(or)

good enough to take a gas jeep and bring back my grandchildren.

MULDOON
Sure.

ELLIE
I'm going with him.

They head for the door. Hammond turns, staring out the windows at the front of the control room.

He's gone pale, and he's sweating, wrapped up in a million thoughts. Behind him, Ray Arnold's voice calls to him, but he doesn't hear it.

ARNOLD
John - - John - -

Hammond leans on his cane, and for the first time he looks like he's actually using it.

ARNOLD (cont'd)
John.

Hammond turns, finally hearing him.

ARNOLD (cont'd)
I can't get Jurassic Park back on line without Dennis Nedry.

108.

"WHERE ARE MY GLASSES? I CAN AFFORD NEW ONES."

—DENNIS NEDRY

ABOVE Dennis Nedry (Wayne Knight) gets caught in a downpour as he races to deliver the stolen embryos.

OPPOSITE TOP A storyboard panel depicts the fate of Nedry's vehicle as he crashes on the way to deliver the stolen goods to the *Anne B.*

OPPOSITE BOTTOM Early concept art by John Bell shows Nedry's jeep stuck in mud as he tries to make his way to the rendezvous.

EXT PARK ROAD - NIGHT
As the rain continues to pour down, a gas-powered jeep ROARS down another park road.

INT JEEP - NIGHT
DENNIS NEDRY drives the jeep as fast as he can in the treacherous conditions. He MUTTERS to himself, shaking his head.

                    NEDRY
        Shoulda been there by now - -
            shoulda been there - -

He hauls it around a corner and looks down, checking his watch. When he looks back up, his eyes go wide.

There's a white wood guard rail fence, right in front of him. He stands on the brakes as hard as he can. The jeep fishtails, skidding out of control in the mud towards the fence.

Nedry hauls the wheel hard to the side to try to control the skid, but the jeep skids off the road, going halfway over the muddied embankment.

                NEDRY (cont'd)
            God damn it!

He drops the car in reverse and hits the gas. The wheels spin, sending mud flying everywhere, but the jeep goes nowhere, just digs in further.

Nedry can't believe it. Frustrated, he gets out of the jeep.

He stops suddenly - he can see another park road, down the sloping embankment, about twenty feet below.

There is a large sign alongside the road. Nedry leans forward excitedly to get a better look. It reads "TO EAST DOCK." He scrambles to the front of the jeep.

ON THE HILLSIDE
Nedry CRANKS a winch from its coil on the front end of the jeep.

> **NEDRY**
> (mumbling to himself)
>
> No problem. Winch this sucker off the thing - - tie it to a thing - - pull it down the thing - - and pull it back up.

He loses his balance and slips - falling back on his rear. He slides down the muddy embankment, across the road below. Pissed, he gets to his knees and searches for his glasses.

> **NEDRY (cont'd)**
> Where are my glasses? I can afford new ones.

THE SPITTER

The *Dilophosaurus* scene in which Nedry meets a grisly death largely remained set in stone from the novel across the various drafts. "The Spitter was an obvious choice to put in the film," remarks Scotch Marmo. "He caught my attention as a fabulously visual and eerily scary beast. He just invokes crazy dinosaur that an audience will talk about later. Even his name was great: The Spitter." Crichton's account of Nedry's death in the novel is particularly horrifying, as the traitorous coder, blinded by the Spitter's venom, feels a sharp pain in his belly before realizing with horror that "he was holding his own intestines in his hands."

The violence was toned down across the screenplay iterations. In Crichton's first draft, the blinded Nedry gropes his way to the jeep, only to get pulled away by the dinosaur, "his fingernails clawing at the fabric of the seat." The revised draft sees the addition of a sightless Nedry smacking his head on the frame of the vehicle, an element that was retained in both Scotch Marmo's and Koepp's drafts. In Koepp's first draft, Nedry tries to shoo away the creature like a dog, even throwing rocks at it—in the final draft, he would throw a stick for the dinosaur. Koepp's final draft also features alternate dialogues for Nedry, including a moment where he calls the dinosaur a "lame brain" and a "walnut brain . . . extinct kangaroo," although none of these insults made the finished film.

Crichton's screenplay drafts also included a moment where Nedry's corpse is discovered by Muldoon and Gennaro, surrounded by Compys, his "boyish face red and bloated." Scotch Marmo riffed on this, with Muldoon and two workers finding Nedry, or rather bits of him, scattered across the park.

He stands and grabs the winch, and goes to a sturdy-looking tree on the other side.

> NEDRY (cont'd)
> You can make it!

From the distance, there is a soft HOOTING sound. There's some movement in the bushes - Nedry looks around for the source of the sound and movement. He doesn't find it. He nervously checks his watch and goes back to the winch, but faster.

> NEDRY (cont'd)
> No problem - - pop this thing right down - -

The HOOTING comes again and Nedry turns - again, nothing.

A figure ducks around the tree and pops out on the other side, HOOTING playfully.

Nedry looks around one side of the tree - nothing. It pops up on the other side, HOOTING again. And Nedry looks again. Nothing. It seems like a friendly game of hide-and-seek. But Nedry begins to get rattled.

                    NEDRY
        That's nice. Gotta go. I'm
        getting out of here. C'mon you
              can make it!

He secures the winch and starts across the road, back up the embankment. He freezes, as he feels something behind him. He turns around slowly and sees:

A dilophosaur. It stands only about four feet high, is spotted like an owl, and has a brilliant colored crest that flanks its head. It doesn't look very dangerous. In fact, it's kind of cute.

                 NEDRY (cont'd)
        Oh. Uh - - nice boy. Nice boy. Okay.
        Run along. I don't have anything for
          you! Go on! Go home! Dinner time!
          Are you hungry? They'll feed you!
               Go, boy. Girl. Whatever.

The dilophosaur just stares at Nedry, tilting its head curiously. Nedry looks around on the ground and finds a stick. He picks it up and chucks it at the thing. He throws it as far as he can.

                 NEDRY (cont'd)
          Nice juicy stick! Fetch!

The dilophosaur gets into the spirit of the game, but not the object.

                 NEDRY (cont'd)
        Lame brain! What's the matter with
                     you?

                     (or)

        What's the matter with you?

He shakes his head and starts back towards the jeep, muttering to himself.

                 NEDRY (cont'd)
        Walnut brain . . . extinct
        kangaroo . . . hope I run over you
             on the way down - -

- - - - - - - ??-OR-?? - - - - - - -

                 NEDRY (cont'd)
        Walnut brain . . . extinct
        kangaroo . . . hope I run over you
             on the way down - -

He's near the top when the dilophosaur suddenly hops out right in front of him, startling him. Nedry loses his balance and falls back, right on his rear. He gets to his feet, angry.

                 NEDRY (cont'd)
               I said - -

He picks up a stick and chucks it at the thing.

OPPOSITE TOP Nedry (Wayne Knight) comes face-to-face with the *Dilophosaurus*.

OPPOSITE BOTTOM Colorful concept art for the *Dilophosaurus* by Mark "Crash" McCreery.

BELOW A storyboard panel shows a panicked Nedry as the *Dilophosaurus* closes in.

NEDRY (cont'd)
- - beat it!

- - - - - - - - - - - - - - - - - -

NEDRY (cont'd)
What are you do - -

The animals HISSES. The brightly
colored fan around its neck flares
wildly, two bulbous sacs on either
side of its neck inflate. It rears
its head back again - -

- - and it SPITS.

SPLAT! A big glob of something wet
SMACKS into the middle of Nedry's
chest. He reaches down and touches
the goo that's dribbling down his
slicker.

NEDRY (cont'd)
That's disgusting!

SPLAT! Another glob of goo SMACKS
into the headlight, right next to
Nedry's head.

He stands up. A look of confusion

THESE PAGES Storyboards
outline the scene in which
the Spitter blinds Nedry
with its poisonous venom.

crosses his face. He lifts his right hand, the one that he touched the spit with, and looks at it strangely, flexing it.

POW! This time the loogie hits Nedry right smack in the face. He SCREAMS and rubs it away, frantically.

Because it hurts. Like hell. Nedry falls back, clawing at his eyes, in excruciating pain. He pulls his hands away, starting to hyperventilate. He flails his arms in front of him, blinking a mile a minute, but blinded.

He staggers forward, to try to get into the jeep. He gets the door open, but SMACKS his head on the door frame and collapses.

The can of shaving cream flies out of Nedry's jacket pocket - - and tumbles into runoff water, down the muddy hillside. Nedry gets to his feet again and staggers in the general direction of the jeep. He reaches the open door and feels his way in. He SLAMS the door.

There is another HOOT. From inside the jeep.

Nedry turns and SCREAMS. The dilophosaur is right there, in the passenger seat. It HISSES louder than before, its crest fans angrily, vibrating, reaching a crescendo - -

- - and the thing pounces, SLAMMING Nedry back against the driver's window, SHATTERING it. As Nedry shrieks - -

Rain and mud wash over the shaving cream can, burying it.

THESE PAGES Grant to the rescue: Storyboards sketch out the moment the paleontologist climbs the tree to rescue Tim, finding him in the tour vehicle.

As Grant gets rid of the blood, his injury doesn't look so bad, just a gash on his forehead.

He turns and looks up to the tree the Explorer fell in. It's stuck there, nose down in the thickest top branches.

Lex's GASPS are getting louder. She's terrified.

> **GRANT**
> Hey, come on, don't - - don't - - don't - - just - - just - - stop, stop.

He touches her, but it's awfully awkward, more of a pat on the head than anything strong or reassured.

But she responds to the contact, hurling herself forward and throwing her arms tightly around his waist. She clamps here, holding on for dear life, SOBBING.

> **GRANT** (cont'd)
> Lex, you gotta be quiet, please. Stop it. Shhhhh.

This seems to quiet her.

> **GRANT** (cont'd)
> Because if we make too much noise, he's going to hear us and come back.

Lex bursts out crying again, a WAILING scream, nearly hysterical now. Grant holds her, no idea what to do. He turns and looks around.

> **GRANT** (cont'd)
> (a whispered shout)
>
> Timmy?! Timmy!

He hears a CRACKING sound. He looks

EXT PARK GROUNDS - NIGHT
The rain has all but stopped now. GRANT and LEX are at the bottom of the large barrier leading up to the park road. Like it or not, they're in the park now, and are surrounded by thick jungle foliage on all sides. They're both beaten up, and Grant's face is covered in blood.

He's bent over a big puddle, splashing water on his face, rinsing the blood off, and trying to bring himself to.

Poor Lex is scared as hell. She stands behind Grant, ramrod straight, her breath coming in short, desperate GASPS. Her eyes are wide, and she doesn't look like she can move.

up to the tree again. The Explorer
has fallen a few feet lower into the
branches.

Grant looks down at Lex, who is
sitting on a rock.

> **LEX**
> Dad - - Dad - -

> **GRANT**
> Shhh - - I'm right here, Lex. I'm
> going to look after you. I'm going
> to help your brother. I want you to
> stay here and wait for me, okay?

> **LEX**
> He left us! He left us!

> **GRANT**
> That's not what I'm going to do.
> Good!

Grant walks to the tree. Lex
scampers into the culvert.

EXT TREE - NIGHT
GRANT takes a deep breath, grabs
hold of the first branch, and starts
his long climb. Fortunately, it's
a good climbing tree, its branches
thick and regularly spaced.

Grant moves at a good pace. He
reaches the car's level, on the
driver's side five or six feet to one
side of it.

The car's in rough shape. It's much
thinner than it used to be, its nose
completely smashed in, the front wheels
driven solidly into a thick branch.
They are what hold it in place.

> **GRANT**
> Tim? Tim?

Grant comes up to the car and looks
in. TIM is huddled on the floor on
the passenger side, frightened,

hugging his knees to his chest.

He looks up at Grant with a tear and
blood-streaked faced. His voice is
barely audible.

> **TIM**
> I threw up.

> **GRANT**
> That's okay. Listen, give me your
> hand.

Tim doesn't move.

> **GRANT (cont'd)**
> I won't tell anybody you threw up.
> Just give me your hand, okay?

He reaches out. Tim reaches too, but

they're still about a foot apart. Grant grabs hold of the steering wheel, to pull himself further in. The wheel turns.

On the branch, the front wheels turn, losing a bit of their grip on the thick branch they're resting on.

Tim and Grant grab hands. Grant holds on to him, getting an arm securely around his waist. They climb down. They stop on a branch.

> GRANT
> Okay, that's not so bad, ah Tim?

> TIM
> Yes it is.

> GRANT
> It's just like coming out of a tree house. Did your dad ever build you a tree house, Tim, eh?

> TIM
> No.

> GRANT
>
> Me too.
>
> (he starts to move down)
>
> Okay. Well, the main thing about climbing is never, never look down, never.

> TIM
> This is impossible. How am I going . . . I can't make it. This is . . . it's about fifty feet.

> GRANT
> So am I going to help you with your foot?

> TIM
> What if the car falls?

> (or)

> What if the wheels fall?

The car GROANS forward on the branch, which sags in their direction. They look up. The car begins to shift dramatically towards them.

> GRANT
> Oh, no! GO, Tim, go! Go!

They climb down, as fast as they can, as the big branch that is supporting the car CREAKS, ready to give way any second.

> GRANT (cont'd)
> Faster! Faster!

The branch breaks. Disintegrates, really, and the car falls straight at them.

Grant and Tim let go of the branch they're on and fall, THUDDING into another branch a few feet down. The car SMACKS into the big branch they just vacated, and stops there.

Grant and Tim are half climbing, half falling down the tree now, slipping on the resin-covered branches, just trying like hell to get out of the way.

CREEEE-POW! The second branch breaks, and now the car SMASHES and CRASHES through a network of thinner branches, headed right for them. It hits open space and goes into free fall.

Grant turns, and puts up his arms in defense - -

- - and the car stops, SLAMMING into a thick branch just above him.

Grant looks up, eyeball to eyeball with the front grill. The new branch starts to CREAK.

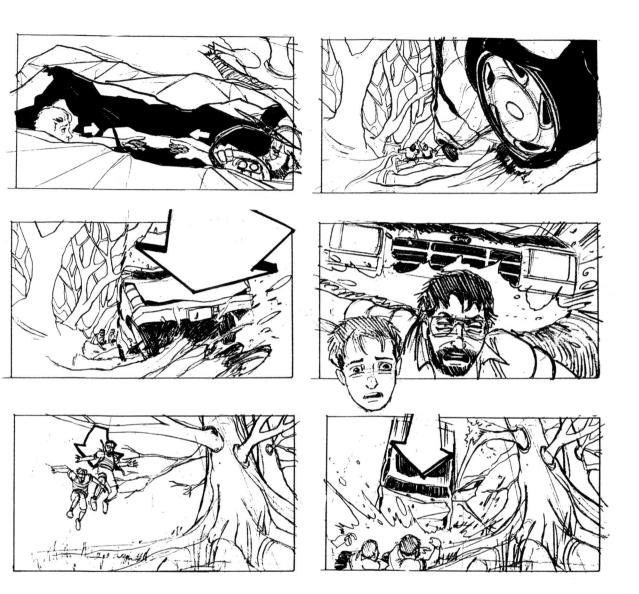

Grant and Tim basically fall down the rest of the tree, the car BASHING its way through right behind them. They jump the last six or seven feet and hit the ground, hard.

Grant grabs Tim and rolls with him, to the side, just as the car SMASHES into the earth, nose first, standing upright that way.

They look up in relief, but the damn thing's still heading for them, now tipping over, falling straight at them, and there's no way they have time to get out of the way this time, so Grant just balls himself up on top of Tim to try to protect him and - -

- - CRASH! The jeep falls on top of them. Grant, amazingly unhurt, looks up confused.

ABOVE Storyboards depict the race against time, as Grant and Tim clamber down the tree and the vehicle comes crashing down after them.

NO JOKE

As David Koepp notes, the final film includes "a very few well-timed and well-executed jokes . . . just very nice tension-breaking jokes." Most of them are delivered by Jeff Goldblum as Dr. Ian Malcolm, for instance: "If the Pirates of the Caribbean breaks down, the pirates don't eat the tourists," a riposte aimed at John Hammond when he attempts to brush aside the chaos that has engulfed his park. Koepp's favorite joke in the movie, however, is delivered by Tim in the scene where the Ford Explorer that he and Grant have just escaped crashes through the branches of the tree they have just climbed down and topples over them. "I do think, 'Well, we're back in the car' is the best one," Koepp says.

ABOVE "We're back in the car": Storyboards show the action that leads to David Koepp's favorite joke in the film, as the tour vehicle lands and tips over, covering Grant and Tim.

They're inside the jeep again, saved by the hole in the sunroof.

CUT TO:

EXT CULVERT - NIGHT
LEX is still in the culvert, terrified, slowly BANGING her head against the wall.

GRANT is at the mouth of the culvert, carefully studying the rinky-dink map of the park he picked up during the slide show.

> GRANT
> Okay - - okay - -

He's trying to get his bearings from the crude, cartoon-like drawing on the map, but it's tough.

He looks up, picking a direction, and shoves the map in his pocket decisively.

He looks back in at Lex.

> GRANT (cont'd)
> Lex, you're going to have to get out of there.
>
> (he walks towards her)

Hiding isn't a rational solution; we have to improve our situation.

She doesn't move. Grant looks at TIM.

> GRANT (cont'd)
> Tim's out here.
>
> (Grant picks Tim up)
>
> He's okay.

Still nothing. Grant tries a new tack.

> GRANT (cont'd)
> (walking away)

'Course you could just wait in there
   while we go back and get help.

                 TIM
           (following Grant)

        That's a good idea.

               GRANT
     You'll probably be safe enough
        (alone) on your own - -

                 TIM
          I doubt it.

               GRANT
     Maybe - - it's hard to say.

               LEX
    Liar! You said you wouldn't leave!

               GRANT
    I'm trying to use psychology to get
     you out of the drain, you know!

She just stares at him like he's
nuts. Tim shakes his head at Grant,
as if to say "nice try." Grant calms
his tone.

- - - - - - - VERSION 1 - - - - - -

            GRANT (cont'd)
    We can't go back the way we came.
    What we have is a free-range T-rex
    on the road. There's (there are)
     fences on either side. If we meet
   him between here and the lodge, we'd
    have problems. But what this means,
   what this means, is that this whole
           paddock is empty.

             It's safe.

               LEX
            It's safe?

               GRANT
             It's safe.

                 LEX
             It's safe.

               GRANT
     Go (and) that's the way we're going
        to go. What do you say?

               LEX
             Alright.

- - - - - - - END - - - - - - - -

- - - - - - VERSION 2 - - - - - -

            GRANT (cont'd)
     Alright. We're just going to walk
       back home. Together.

He walks over to Lex at the culvert
and sits across from her.

            GRANT (cont'd)
     But we can't walk back on the road.
    There are fences on either side. And
     if we meet the Rex between here and
       the lodge we'd - - have problems.

Lex covers her ears. Grant tries to
calm her.

            GRANT (cont'd)
    He's probably staked out the road as
     a feeding ground, which means this
     whole paddock is empty. It's safe.

    It's safe, and that's the way we're
       going to go. What do you say?

- - - - - - - - END - - - - - - -

He's spoken calmly and confidently,
so Lex crawls out of the culvert and
stands next to him.

               GRANT
            Good girl.

He kisses her hand and helps her
crawl out of the culvert.

"IT'S SAFE?"
—LEX MURPHY

Tim and Lex nod, and he starts off in the direction he indicated. They trail behind him.

> **GRANT (cont'd)**
> Might be kind of slow, but it can't be more than three or four miles. I'd hoped the rex finished feeding by now, but let's not kid ourselves. Did you know a carnivore can eat up to 25% of its body weight in (about) one sitting, so he's probably just ready to move on to the main course by now - -

He stops in the middle of the sentence, noticing he's alone. He turns around. Now both Kids have scampered all the way back into the culvert, terrified.

ABOVE A terrified Lex (Ariana Richards) contemplates the horrors she has just witnessed, from the safety of a culvert.

EXT PARK ROAD - NIGHT
MULDOON and ELLIE race down the park road in an open-topped jeep like the one Nedry took earlier. Neither of them speak, they just stare ahead grimly, wondering what they're about to find.

> **MULDOON**
> There they are!

They round a corner and come to the top of the hill, where the attack took place. The jeep skids to a stop and they jump out.

The road is a rutted, muddy mess. The cement block house is a pile of rubble. One of the Explorers is gone, the other stands untouched, both doors hanging open.

ELLIE

    Oh, God. Where's the other car?

She runs to the Explorer. Muldoon
follows, looking around.

AT THE EXPLORER,

Ellie leans in and looks around.
Nobody's there. She and Muldoon
walk towards the wreckage of the
outhouse, calling out:

ELLIE (cont'd)

    I think it's ahead of us.

MULDOON

    It could be anywhere. With the
fences out, it can go in and out of
    any paddock it likes.

They hear a MOANING sound from
somewhere in the wreckage of the
restroom building. They rush over
to it.

IAN MALCOLM lies on his back,
semiconscious among the twisted wood
and cement.

MULDOON

    It's Malcolm!

He shines his light along the length
of Malcolm's body. His shirt is
soaked with blood, but his right leg
is even worse off. The right ankle
is bent outward at a strange angle
from his leg, the trousers flattened,
soaked with blood.

Malcolm's belt has been twisted
around his thigh.

ELLIE

  He's put a tourniquet on. Dr. Ian!
         Dr. Ian!

Malcolm GROANS as she touches him,
groggy.

MALCOLM

  Remind me to thank John for a lovely
        weekend.

The T-rex ROARS again. But closer
now. Ellie and Muldoon look at each
other.

ELLIE

    Can we chance moving him?

MALCOLM

    Please - - chance it.

Muldoon lays Malcolm as carefully as
possible in the back of the jeep.

MALCOLM

    Where are the kids?

Ellie looks around.

ELLIE

    Lex! Tim!

She turns and looks back at the
empty road. She's on the verge of
tears, but is fighting them back.

MULDOON

    Dr. Sattler, I've seen a lot
   of animal attacks. People just
   disappear. No blood, no trace.
    That's the way it happens.

ELLIE

    No, no, no!

She walks to the edge of the road,
her eyes following the deep ruts
the Explorer made when it went over
the edge. Muldoon gets ready to
leave.

MULDOON

    Ellie, come on!!

ELLIE

    The other car!

ABOVE Sattler (Laura Dern), an injured Malcolm (Jeff Goldblum), and Muldoon (Bob Peck) realize they're not alone on the Main Road, as the T. rex comes back for seconds.

EXT CLEARING - NIGHT
ELLIE's and MULDOON's flashlight beams spray light by the base of the tree.

> **MULDOON**
> Dr. Grant!

> **ELLIE**
> Alan!

They find the wrecked Explorer. Muldoon peers inside, looking for anything.

> **ELLIE**
> Do you see anything?

> **MULDOON**
> I don't know.

The T-rex ROARS again, closer still.

Ellie nervously goes to the other side of the car and looks in.

> **ELLIE**
> Alan?!

He looks down, at one of the T-rex footprints in the road. It's filled with water.

The water in the puddle vibrates rhythmically. Malcolm's eyes widen. He looks around, frantically.

> MALCOLM
> Uh - - anybody? Anybody hear that?

EXT CLEARING - NIGHT
ELLIE is still looking around, to MULDOON's chagrin. Her flashlight falls on three sets of footprints in the mud.

> ELLIE
> Look!

With her flashlight, she follows the trail the footprints made. They lead into the jungle and disappear.

EXT PARK ROAD - NIGHT
MALCOLM's staring, wide-eyed, at the rings in the water, which are getting bigger now.

> MALCOLM
> It's a - - an impact tremor is what it is, it, uh - -

BOOM. BOOM.

> MALCOLM (cont'd)
> I'm fairly alarmed here!

ELLIE and MULDOON come up over the embankment, excited.

> MALCOLM
> Gotta move, gotta get out of here. Let's go - we gotta go, we gotta get out of here, right now! Go, go! Let's hurry, let's get out of here!

> MULDOON
> They're not here.

Ellie desperately searches the ground for any signs of Grant. She finds their footprints.

> ELLIE (o.s.)
> Thank God.

EXT PARK ROAD - NIGHT
MALCOLM, laid out in the back of the jeep, feels something strange.

"GOGOGOGOGOGOGOGOGOGO!"
—IAN MALCOLM

They stop talking. The BOOMING is louder now, and faster. Much faster. They look back, over their shoulders.

> **ELLIE**
> Oh.

Ellie and Muldoon get into the jeep, Muldoon in the driver's seat.

ABOVE As Sattler, Malcolm, and Muldoon escape in a jeep, the T. rex gives chase.

OPPOSITE Early storyboards depict the T. rex in pursuit of the escaping jeep.

> **MALCOLM**
> Move now! Let's go, let's go, right now, right now!

The tyrannosaur SMASHES out of the jungle foliage, bursts onto the road, and runs straight at them, moving at least thirty miles an hour.

> **MALCOLM**
> GOGOGOGOGOGOGOGOGOGO!

Muldoon fumbles for the keys, turns the jeep over, and SLAMS it into gear. He drops the clutch, hits the gas, and tears ass out of there.

But the jeep is slow to work through the first few gears. Terrified, Ellie dares to look down, to the side view mirror, which tells her "Objects Are Closer Than They Appear."

And they sure are. The T-rex is still gaining on the slowly accelerating jeep. All three of them stare back at the rex in terror –

ELLIE
Faster, faster!

MALCOLM
Must go faster, it's getting closer -
must go faster!

ELLIE
Faster! Shit, shit, shit, faster!

MALCOLM
Must go faster, go, go. Open it up,
5th gear, 5th gear! Here it comes!
Stand on it! Fifth - stand on it, 5th
gear, go!

- - which means they don't see the
half-fallen tree branch right in
front of them, blocking the path of
the road. Muldoon looks back first,
SHOUTS - -

MULDOON
DOWN!

- - they all duck.

The windshield hits the branch and
SHATTERS as the jeep flies ahead,
really picking up speed now.

The T-rex just runs right through
the branch, SMASHING it entirely.

They're bounced around pretty
badly. Malcolm is knocked into the
front, and in so doing knocks the
gear shift into neutral. The engine
RACES, the T-rex closes in again - -

Losing ground now, the dinosaur
makes a final lunge for the jeep and
CRUNCHES into the left rear quarter
panel - -

ELLIE
Faster, faster!

- - but Muldoon SLAMS it back into

THESE PAGES Storyboards
depict the nerve-wracking
moment in which the
T. rex closes in on the jeep.

gear and guns it. The T-rex gives
up, fading into the distance.

They drive in silence for a few
moments, all scared out of their
wits.

                MALCOLM
   Think they'll have that on the tour?

EXT PARK GROUND - NIGHT
GRANT, LEX, and TIM make their way
through Jurassic Park. Far in the
distance, there's another ROAR. Grant
hears it, but tries not to show it.

                 LEX
             Hear that?

                (or)

        Are you hearing this?

                GRANT
        No, I didn't hear anything.

                (or)

            No, we're okay.

They keep walking, but now Grant
is looking around for a safe place
to hide. He looks up, to the
towering trees around them.

              GRANT (cont'd)
        You (guys) both look pretty tired. I
                 think

                (or)

          why don't we find

                (or)

      we ought to find someplace to rest.

He hears another ROAR.

GRANT (cont'd)
Like about now. C'mon! Hurry up!
Like this tree.

LEX
Why are we hurrying if there's
nothing wrong?

TIM
What if we fall? I hate trees.

EXT TREE - NIGHT
LEX, TIM, and GRANT climb. Grant
is behind, watching the other two,
giving them a push up when they need
it.

TIM
I hate trees!

LEX
They don't bother me.

TIM
Yeah, you weren't in that last one.

Now, near the top of the tree, the
three of them sit there, dangling
their legs, looking out over the
park.

It's an incredible view. They can
see in all directions. And with the
full moon, there's a lot of detail.

Most striking of all are dozens of
sauropod heads, at the end of long
necks, that tower over the park.

TIM (cont'd)
Hey! Those are brontosauruses - - I
mean, those are brachiosauruses.

GRANT
It's okay to call them brontosaurs,
Tim. It's a great name. It's a
romantic name. It means "thunder
lizard."

TIM
(digging that)

"Thunder lizard!"

Grant finds a solid web of branch
and settles himself in it, leaning
back against the trunk of the tree,
with a little room on either side of
him. Lex nestles up next to him on
the branch. Grant is surprised, but
accepts it.

Tim climbs off to the side, to a
nook in the branch of his own.

Silent for a moment, the three can
hear the HOOTS of the animals as
they call. Some are almost musical.

GRANT
Listen to that! They're singing!

(he moves over to a higher branch)

Of course no one's ever heard one
from a dinosaur before, but - - I
could swear that sounds suspiciously
to me like a mating call (to me). In
an all-female environment - -

(or)

On an all-girl island?

He smiles, enchanted. He HOOTS
himself, trying to imitate one of
the calls. Immediately, five or
six of the heads turn in their
direction and HOOT back.

LEX
No, no, sh, sh, sh - - stop! Stop!
Stop! Don't let the monsters come
over here!

GRANT
They're not monsters, Lex. They're
just animals. And these are
herbivores.

TIM
That means they only eat vegetables. But for you, I think they'd make an exception.

GRANT
Tim, Tim, Tim . . .

LEX
Oh, I hate the other kind.

GRANT
They're just doing what they do.

(or)

Well the other kind - -

(he gets off the branch and goes back to sit with the Kids)

- - just do what they do.

LEX
Dorkatops!

TIM
Straight-A brainiac!

GRANT
Could you guys possibly cool that for a - -

Satisfied, Tim settles in for the night. Grant shifts too, getting comfortable, but something in his pocket pinches him. He winces and digs it out. It's the velociraptor claw he unearthed so long ago in Montana.

Yesterday, actually. He looks at it, thinking a million thoughts, staring at this thing that used to be so priceless.

LEX
What are you gonna do now if you don't have to dig up dinosaur bones anymore?

FATHER FIGURE

One of the biggest changes to Alan Grant's character that came in the transition from the novel to the screen is his attitude toward children. In Crichton's book, Grant is enthusiastic: "Grant liked kids—it was impossible not to like any group so openly enthusiastic about dinosaurs." In Koepp's final draft, Grant experiences an evolution, expressing his dislike of kids at the start, but becoming a surrogate father by the end. "That came on in subsequent drafts," explains Koepp. "You don't have a lot of time in these [films] for personal stories and traditional character arcs. It's about establishing who are these people in a few deft strokes, and how might that change as the movie goes on." In Koepp's drafts, Grant is shown to be a commitment-phobe. "It doesn't go with his lifestyle at all," says Koepp. "I mean the thing is with kids, you adapt your lifestyle, and you make it work. He could dig for bones in the desert and have kids. But it seems unfathomable to him. Because his work is everything. And that would just change it. And so it's probably hard to get his head around."

TOP A storyboard panel shows Grant and the kids observing a group of *Brachiosaurs* in wonder.

OPPOSITE TOP Sattler arrives at the Jurassic Park Visitor Center restaurant to join John Hammond for ice cream.

GRANT
I guess we'll just have to evolve too.

TIM
What do you call a blind dinosaur?

GRANT
I don't know. What do you call a blind dinosaur?

TIM
A Do-you-think-he-saurus. What do you call a blind dinosaur's dog?

GRANT
You got me.

TIM
A Do-you-think-he-saurus Rex.

Grant laughs. Both Kids finally close their eyes, but after a moment, Lex pops hers open again.

LEX
What if the dinosaur comes back while we're all asleep?

GRANT
I'll stay awake.

LEX
(skeptical)

All night?

GRANT
All night.

Grant lets the claw fall to the ground.

INT RESTAURANT - NIGHT

ELLIE comes into the darkened restaurant, following the source of the flickering light. A candle burns at a table in the corner.

JOHN HAMMOND sits at the table, alone. There is a bucket of ice cream in the middle, and he's eating a dish of it, staring down morosely.

Ellie draws up to the table and Hammond looks up at her. His eyes are puffy, his hair is messed up - - for the first time we've seen him, the fire is gone from his eyes.

> HAMMOND
> They were all melting.

> (or)

> It was all melting.

Ellie just nods.

> ELLIE
> Malcolm's okay for now. I gave him a shot of morphine.

> HAMMOND
> They'll all be fine. Who better to get the children through Jurassic Park than a dinosaur expert?

Ellie nods. Another pause. Hammond breaks it again.

> HAMMOND (cont'd)
> You know the first attraction I ever built when I came down south from Scotland? Was a Flea Circus, Petticoat Lane. Really quite wonderful. We had a wee trapeze, a roundabout - - a merry-go - - what you call it?

BORN SHOWMAN

The idea of Hammond eating ice cream as Jurassic Park goes off the rails was created by Scotch Marmo. In her draft, the scene features him talking to Muldoon, referring to the ensuing chaos as "a little breakdown from the storm or whatever." He's in complete denial, says the writer: "His park is falling apart all around him, but he is not willing to see it." In Koepp's first draft, Hammond shares ice cream with Sattler, realizing during their conversation that she is in love with Grant when she says: "Alan's a strong man—strong and smart. If anyone can make it back, he can." Koepp's handwritten notes on the draft crossed out the first part of the sentence, changing it to: "Alan's too much of a show-off to die. He's strong." Hammond then asks: "Did I play God?" to which Sattler replies: "That's between you and Him." The scene was later expanded. "That was rewritten during shooting as I recall," says Koepp. "That was one of those scenes that got heavily rewritten. There's one in every movie that ends up being written twenty-five times because they're usually that kind of scene. Sort of pivotal, sort of quiet, sort of delicate. And I remember that was with input from Laura. And Sir Richard, and Steven and me. That was the scene that we chewed over quite a bit. I think Steven wanted to alter the pace and tone at that point, which was a very nice decision."

The final version riffs on an idea from Crichton's novel, in which Hammond is called "flamboyant, a born showman." In Koepp's rewrite, Hammond talks about the first attraction he built when he came from Scotland to London's Petticoat Lane: a flea circus, complete with trapeze and carousel. The novel features another piece of circus-themed backstory for Hammond, who in 1983, with the help of a Stanford geneticist, bred a miniature elephant, using a dwarf-elephant embryo that was raised in an artificial womb. Standing just nine inches high, the creature was held in a cage and unveiled to potential investors—as he sought money for his genetics company, International Genetic Technologies, Inc. "He's a bit of a huckster," says Koepp.

ELLIE
Carousel.

HAMMOND
A carousel - - and a seesaw. They
all moved, motorized of course, but
people would swear they could see
the fleas. "I see the fleas, mummy!
Can't you see the fleas?" Clown fleas,
high wire fleas, fleas on parade . . .

(he trails off)

Ellie just looks at him, not sure
what his state is. He goes on.

HAMMOND (cont'd)
But with this place, I - - I wanted
to give (show) them something real,
something that wasn't an illusion,
something they could see and (feel)
touch. An aim devoid of (without)
merit.

ELLIE
But you can't think through this
one. You have to feel it.

HAMMOND
You're absolutely right. Yes, you're
right. Hiring Nedry was a mistake,
that's obvious. We're over-dependent
on automation, I can see that now.
But that's all correctable for the
next time around.

ELLIE
John, John. John, you're still
building onto that Flea Circus, that
illusion. And now you're adding onto
it by what you're doing here. That's
the illusion.

HAMMOND
(When) Once we have control again
we - -

ELLIE
Control?! You never had control!
I was overwhelmed by the power of
this place. So I made a mistake
too. I didn't have enough respect
for that power, and it's out now.
You're sitting here trying to pick
up the pieces. John, there's nothing

> ## "BUT YOU CAN'T THINK THROUGH THIS ONE. YOU HAVE TO FEEL IT."
> —ELLIE SATTLER

worth picking up. The only thing that matters now are the people we love. Alan, Lex, and Tim. And John, they're out there where people are dying - - people are dying, you know?

There is a long pause. Hammond avoids her gaze. Ellie reaches out and takes a spoon out of one of the buckets of ice cream, and licks it. Finally:

> ELLIE (cont'd)
> It's good.

He looks up at her, and his face is different, as the unhappy irony of what he's about to say finally hits home.

> HAMMOND
> Spared no expense.

ABOVE Concept art by David J. Negrón shows Lex riding the baby *Triceratops* that she dubs Ralph, while Tim feeds juvenile *Brachiosaurs* from a tree.

EXT PARK - DAWN
The sun comes up over Jurassic Park. The danger of the night before is overcome by the sheer beauty of the place - - it really is like the Serengeti Plain.

Over at the edge of a great open field, a huge tree marks the border between the open area and the thick of the jungle.

UP IN THE TREE,
GRANT, TIM, and LEX are asleep in the branches of the tree, both Kids now curled up under Grant's arms.

A heavy shadow falls over all three of them, blocking out the sun entirely. Grant awakens, only a little bit asleep, as - -

ABOVE Early storyboards show Tim feeding dinosaurs. **OPPOSITE** Lex encounters a baby *Triceratops*, a sequence that came close to being filmed but was dropped for budgetary reasons at the last minute.

- - a brachiosaur's head pushes into the tree branches, right up beside them. It hesitates there for a second, seemingly staring at them. Grant just watches as it opens its mouth very wide and CHOMPS down on a branch over their heads.

The Kids awaken with a start. Tim points, Lex opens her mouth to scream, but nothing comes out. Then - -

                    LEX
                Go away!

                    GRANT
                (quietly)

    It's okay! It's okay! It's a
            brachiosaur!

THE YOUNG TRIKE

In the novel, after the *T. rex* attack, Grant and his charges find shelter in a concrete building, bedding down in the hay for the night. The following morning, Lex is seen riding a baby *Triceratops* that she christens Ralph. "Because he looks like Ralph. At school," she reasons. For a long time, it was a staple sequence in the various screenplay iterations, with Spielberg fully intending to film it. The scene features in the Crichton drafts (in the first, she refers to the creature as Ralph; in the revised draft, she doesn't). In Scotch Marmo's take, Lex tumbles off the Trike and falls into a stream. "I can't swim," she yells, as Tim dives in after her—only to discover that she's standing in just a foot of water. In Koepp's first draft, he moved the scene earlier in the story, when the party discovers the sick adult *Triceratops*. Temporarily Lex disappears, only to suddenly materialize riding the creature. The baby Trike scene was intended to be in the film right up until production, with Stan Winston Studio even building a five-foot baby Trike. Ultimately, however, the scene was cut for financial reasons, shaving $500,000 off the budget.

THESE PAGES Storyboards
show Lex riding Ralph,
the baby Triceratops, and
taking a tumble from
the dinosaur's back.

                    TIM
        Veggiesaurus, Lex, Veggiesaurus!

But Lex isn't taking any chances and
scrambles back, away from its mouth.
Tim and Grant come together on the
branch, just staring at the dinosaur
in wonder as it eats its breakfast.

Grant gets another branch.

Tim scampers up, trying to get the
brachiosaur's attention.

                 TIM (cont'd)
        Come here, boy - - I mean girl.

            (he tries whistling)

Grant moves forward and tries to
feed the brachiosaur. The animal
gets the end of the branch and
starts a tug-of-war with Grant.

Tim tries to help him - - they
really begin to have a good time
with the brachiosaur.

HONK! The brachiosaur makes a loud
honking noise, startling Grant and
the Kids.

                   GRANT
        Take a bite, take a bite. I'm not
                letting go.

TIM
It's so strong! Look at its nose.

(he grabs onto the branch)

Need help?

Tim reaches out, petting the
dinosaur's head while it chews.

TIM (cont'd)
That's a girl. Hey Lex, you can
touch it. It's a girl, just like
you. Come on, it's okay. Lex, come
on and touch it. It likes you. It's
gotta like you. Come on Lex. Lex,
come over and touch - - it's a girl,
it has to like you. Lex, why don't
you touch it. It has to like you.
It's a girl.

GRANT
Come on, try some. Take a bite.

TIM
It's good protein. Come on, Lex.
Why don't you touch it? Look at his
nose.

GRANT
This is a seventy-seven ton animal.
Come on over, Lex! Just think of it
as a big cow. Look at its teeth?

(he moves in closer)

Come here, girl. This is a seventy-
seven ton animal. Just think of it
as a big cow!

Grant maneuvers in closer. He
reaches out and grabs hold of the
thing's lip with both hands and
pulls it down, revealing the jaw at
work.

LEX
I like cows.

GRANT

You're a beautiful big animal.

TIM

His nose is running. It looks like
it has a cold.

The dinosaur keeps chewing, not
objecting to the inspection.

TIM

Did you smell that?

Lex tentatively edges forward in the
tree to the inspection.

LEX

Come on girl, up here.

She barely touches the thing on the
tip of its nose - -

- - and it SNEEZES. It's a vast
explosion, and Lex falls back,
dripping wet from head to toe.

TIM

God bless you!

ON THE GROUND,

Lex, her shirt is soaked, and
face all wet, walks away from the
tree. Tim and Grant follow.

TIM

Oh, great. Now she'll never try
anything new!

Lex is embarrassed and ticked off.

BABY MAMA

In Rick Carter's working document, he introduced a scene in which Lex discovers a baby raptor with an injured claw in the park's lava fields. Grant puts the creature in his jacket, strapped to his chest like a sling. He and the children then discover a raptor den hidden in a storm drain and return the baby raptor to its parents. "The lava field I think was an idea that I had because we were going to go over to Hawaii to film," explains Carter. "We didn't want to go all the way to Costa Rica. And they have lava fields on the Big Island, and it just seemed like a natural way to make it seem prehistoric and mysterious."

> TIM (cont'd)
> She'll just sit in her room and never come out and play with her computer - -
>
> LEX
> (as she wipes off some of the wet and throws it at Tim)
>
> I'm a hacker!
>
> TIM
> That's what I said! You're a nerd! They don't call you people hackers anymore - - they call you people nerds!

Tim and Lex continue talking, oblivious to Grant, who has stopped by a tree root trunk.

> TIM
> Hey Lex, ahhhchooo!

> (or)
>
> Hey Lex, come here.
>
> LEX
> What?
>
> TIM
> Hey Lex, you forgot to say gesundheit.

ABOVE Concept art by Tom Cranham shows Grant and the kids carefully picking their way across lava fields, an early idea that didn't make the final film.

OPPOSITE BOTTOM In another concept discarded during the script writing process, a storyboard panel shows Grant discovering a raptor den secreted in a storm drain.

RIVER THRILLER

The journey back to the Visitor Center taken by Grant and the kids differs considerably in the novel and early script drafts to the route they take in Koepp's final screenplay. In the novel, Crichton has the trio take a trip down the river on a rubber raft, drifting past a slumbering *T. rex* at one point. Lex sneezes, waking up the creature, which charges into the water. It eventually relents when it spots a juvenile *T. rex* on the riverbank and goes to investigate. There is no such distraction in the Crichton screenplay drafts, however. In his first draft, the *T. rex* goes under the water, then bucks the raft up in the air, knocking Grant unconscious on a tree branch, although the current ultimately ferries the vessel away from the *T. rex*'s grasp.

Crichton's second draft is even more dramatic: At one point the inflatable raft spins toward the jaws of the dinosaur, until the creature keels over at the last minute, rendered unconscious by a tranquilizer fired by Muldoon on the shore. Scotch Marmo gave a slightly different take on the river scene, with Grant and the kids floating down increasingly dangerous rapids toward a man-made waterfall. As Grant grabs an overhanging branch, stopping the raft from toppling over the waterfall, the water suddenly diminishes, as pumps grind to a halt, with Grant surmising that the power must have been cut. Ultimately, the river ride was jettisoned from the film. "It felt like a delightful and action-packed mini adventure that took the story sideways," Scotch Marmo reflects. "It did not push the story forward." Practically, it was also very expensive. "That whole river sequence that's in the book was a very elaborate sequence, cost a lot of money," says Rick Carter. "Steven was taking on the responsibility for the overall budget, and so he really wanted to condense everything the best he could. I put together memos about how, if he trimmed back certain things, [what] that would cost. And as I remember, that was a $12 million sequence. And we didn't even know exactly how we would do it."

LEFT Concept art by Tom Cranham depicts an unrealized sequence in which Grant and the kids attempt to escape the attentions of the *T. rex* by taking to the river.

THESE PAGES Storyboards illustrate a Crichton story idea in which
Grant and the kids encounter a slumbering *T. rex*.

PAGES 186–187 Storyboards from the abandoned river sequence show Grant, Tim, and
Lex's arrival at the dock as they inflate a raft and use it to float away from the *T. rex*.

NUMBER CRUNCHED

In Koepp's final draft, Grant discovers a batch of hatched dinosaur eggs out in the park, suggesting that life has indeed found a way: The dinosaurs are breeding. In the novel, it plays out differently. Grant discovers a shell fragment from what he believes is a *Velociraptor* egg. Hammond dismisses the find, and the implication that the dinosaurs are breeding, believing the shell fragment is from a bird egg. Arnold, however, realizes there's a serious flaw in their dinosaur counting methodology. The park's computer system has been programmed to count the expected number of dinosaurs, 238, because Dr. Wu and his geneticists were firm in their belief that the dinosaurs, who were all engineered to be female, would not be able to breed. When Arnold changes the tracking parameters, the computer calculates there are now 292 dinosaurs present in the park, confirming Grant's find.

Crichton's drafts included this revelatory story beat, as did Rick Carter's working document. "It just means that the best systems can't track life," says Carter. "That would have been a perfect example of reading something in the book and going 'Well, I think that's a really good idea.'" However, although Koepp's drafts dropped the digital tally, Spielberg took the overall idea even further: Grant, in the film, finds both the discarded eggshell and tiny footprints leading off into the distance. "That's Steven's evolving idea," adds Carter. "You see the egg and you see the little footprints leaving . . . and life will find a way."

Grant is still crouching on the ground below the tree where he landed, staring at something in the palm of his hand. They both come and look over his shoulder, curious. They stare in amazement - -

- - at a whole clutch of dinosaur eggs! All hatched, now empty. Grant picks up one of the fragments, a large one - nearly half an egg.

> **GRANT**
> You know what this is? It's a dinosaur egg. The dinosaurs are breeding.

> **TIM**
> (taking the shell from him)

> But - - my grandpa said all the dinosaurs were girls.

> **GRANT**
> Amphibian.

LEX
What's that?

GRANT
Well, on the tour - - the film said
they used frog DNA to fill in the
gene sequence gaps. They mutated
the dinosaur's genetic code and
blended it with that of frogs. Now,
some West African frogs have been
known to spontaneously change sex
from male to female, in a single
sex environment. Malcolm was right!
Look, life found a way!

INT CONTROL ROOM - DAY
The mood in the room is hopeless.
MALCOLM, his wounds bandaged, but
in real pain, hangs around with
ELLIE and MULDOON, hoping for some
development while RAY ARNOLD is still
at the computer terminal and looking
a mess, he doggedly sorts through
the computer system's lines of code.
One. By one. By one. They BLIP by,
reflected in his glasses. He turns and
stares up at HAMMOND with a look of
absolute incredulity on his face.

ARNOLD
No, no, no, that's crazy, you're out
of your mind, he's absolutely out of
his mind - -

ELLIE
Wait a minute. What exactly does
this mean? Hammond turns to her, the
twinkle back in his eye.

HAMMOND
We're talking, my dear, about a
calculated risk, which is the only
option left to us. We will never
find the command Nedry used. He
covered his tracks far too well, and
I think it's obvious he's not coming
back. So

shutting down the system - -

ARNOLD
I will not do it. You'll have to get
somebody else, because I will not.

HAMMOND
- - shutting down the system is the
only way to guarantee wiping out
everything he did. If I understand
correctly, all the systems will come
back on in their original start-up
modes correct?

ARNOLD
Theoretically, yeah (yes), but we've
never shut down the whole system. It
may not come back at all.

ELLIE
But would we get the phones back?

ARNOLD
Yeah, again, in theory, but - -

MULDOON
(desperate)

What about the lysine contingency?
We could put that into effect!

ELLIE
What's that?

HAMMOND
It's absolutely out of the question.

Hammond walks away from the group.

ARNOLD
The lysine contingency - it's
intended to prevent the spread of
the animals in case they ever got
off the island, but we could use
it now. Dr. Wu inserted a gene that
makes a single faulty enzyme in
protein metabolism. Animals can't
manufacture the amino acid lysine.
Unless they're continually supplied
with lysine by us, they'll go into a
coma and die.

OPPOSITE TOP Grant (Sam
Neill, *left*), accompanied
by Tim (Joseph Mazzello)
and Lex (Ariana Richards),
realizes the dinosaurs on Isla
Nublar have been breeding.

ELLIE
How would we cut off the lysine?

ARNOLD
No trick to it. Just stop running
the program. Leaving them
unattended.

Malcolm speaks up.

MALCOLM
How soon before they become
comatose?

ARNOLD
It would be totally painless - -
they'd just slip into
unconsciousness and they die.

MALCOLM
How long before they slip into
unconsciousness?

ARNOLD
About - - seven days, more or less.

ELLIE
Seven days?! Seven days?! Oh, great.
Oh good - - clever.

MALCOLM
That'll - it'd be a first; man and
dinosaur all die together. John's
plan.

(he raises a hand)

Hammond finally loses his cool. He
BELLOWS, summoning every ounce of
authority at his command. And that's
quite a bit.

HAMMOND
PEOPLE ARE DYING!

There is a moment in which no one dares
to speak. Hammond regains himself.

HAMMOND (cont'd)
Will you please shut down the
system.

Arnold swallows and gets to his feet.

ARNOLD
You asked for it - -

He walks slowly across the room to a
red metal box on the wall. He takes
a key from his belt, unlocks the
door, and opens it.

There is a row of four switches
inside. He flips them off, one by
one, leaving only a single lever
left.

His hand hovers over it . . . and he
flips the lever.

ARNOLD (cont'd)
- - and you got it.

Every monitor, every terminal, every
fluorescent light shuts out, plunging
them into near-darkness.

They just sit in eerie stillness for
a moment.

ELLIE
(hushed voice)

How long will this take?

ARNOLD
'Bout thirty seconds.

They wait, in tense silence.
Hammond adjusts the wilting silk
handkerchief in his breast pocket.
He notices Malcolm staring at him,
his eyes full of disapproval.

HAMMOND
I think perhaps I'll just sit down. I
don't suppose you think all that much
of me now, do you?

MALCOLM
You're all right, John. You're
okay. It's just you don't
have intelligence. You have

"thintelligence." You think narrowly and call it "being focused." You don't see the consequences. You're very good at solving problems, at getting answers - - but you just don't know the right questions.

                  ELLIE
                  Ian - -

Malcolm looks at her.

                  MALCOM
                  Yes?

                  ELLIE
            - - shut up.

                 MALCOLM
                  Yes.

            (to Hammond)

      It's not a criticism, by
             the way.

Finally, Arnold turns back to the box. He flips the row of safety switches back again, then hesitates by the main switch.

                 ARNOLD
      Hold on to your butts.

He throws it. And nothing happens. There is a very long pause.

                 MALCOLM
      It's not working.

                 ARNOLD
                  Uh - -

                MULDOON
   Listen, which of you knows how to
           handle a gun?

Arnold, who can't quite understand this, races over to the main monitor.

RE-BUTT-AL

"Hold onto your butts" remains one of the most quotable lines in *Jurassic Park*, delivered with typical élan by Samuel L. Jackson. First uttered when Arnold initiates the tour program, he repeats it when, later in the film, he reboots the park's systems. The line was not in the original novel, but came courtesy of Koepp, who first heard it from director Robert Zemeckis, with whom he'd just worked on *Death Becomes Her*. "We were doing some reshoots on *Death Becomes Her* to change the ending because the original ending hadn't worked very well for an audience," says Koepp. With the release date looming, the production was under pressure to nail the reshoots quickly. "As the lights went down to watch the dailies of our one and only shot at the new ending, Zemeckis said, 'Hold on to your butts.' And I went back to my office that afternoon and wrote it into the *Jurassic Park* script because I thought 'That's a great line. I love that!'"

                 ARNOLD
           (joyously)

HAH! It's okay! It's okay! Look! See
        that?! LOOK!

They stare at the monitor, which glows with a faint amber light, the only mechanical thing in the room that's on. The left hand corner of the screen displays two words - -

/system ready.

Arnold looks at them, his face triumphant.

ARNOLD (cont'd)
It's on! It worked!

HAMMOND
That will teach you to trust Grandpa.

MALCOLM
Wait a minute? What do you mean "worked"? Everything is still off!

ARNOLD
The shutdown must have tripped the circuit breakers. All we have to do is turn them back on, reboot a few systems in here - - the phones, security doors, half a dozen others - - but it worked! System ready!

MULDOON
Where are the breakers?

GALLIMIMUS

ARNOLD
Out in the maintenance shed. Other side of the compound. I'll go out there. Three minutes, and I can have the power back on in the entire park.

HAMMOND
Just to be safe, I'd like to have everybody in the emergency bunker until Mr. Arnold returns, and the whole system is back on its feet again.

CUT TO:

EXT COMPOUND - DAY
MULDOON and ELLIE carry a jerry-rigged stretcher with MALCOLM on it down a narrow path in the compound. HAMMOND is with them.

CUT TO:

EXT PARK GROUNDS - DAY
GRANT, TIM, and LEX walk through the park grounds, heading across a relatively open area. Grant consults the map.

TIM & LEX
I'm tired, and I'm hungry. When I get back I'm gonna have peanuts and . . . etc.

GRANT
The visitor's center should be just about a mile beyond that rise. If we keep - -

The ANIMAL CRY they heard earlier is closer now, louder, and repeated by many more animals. Grant looks up.

GRANT (cont'd)
What is that? Can you tell me what they are?

TIM
Gallimimus.

He turns around, to face the direction the sound is coming from.

He squints. The ANIMAL CRIES are much louder now, accompanied by a low rumble.

> TIM (cont'd)
> Here - - they're flocking this way.

Grant takes a few steps forward. As he watches, he can make out shapes in the distance.

Dinosaurs. Dozens of them. All at once, he figures it out.

> GRANT
> STAMPEDE!

And that's exactly what it is, a stampede of at least forty dinosaurs, Gallimimus by name. Lex is ready to get out of there, but Grant and Tim hesitate, staring.

The dinosaurs kick up a flock of birds, which startles them, and they all change direction at once, the same way.

> GRANT (cont'd)
> Look at the wheeling - - the uniform direction change! Like a flock of birds evading a predator!

Sure enough, they hear a ROAR, the very familiar roar - -

- - of Tyrannosaurus rex.

> GRANT
> Oh, shit.

Grant and the Kids whirl at the sound, but can't place it, as it seems to come from all around them. They look back towards the stampede. The herd spontaneously changes direction again, and now they're headed straight at them.

The three of them take off, across the meadow, toward the relative cover of the jungle. It's a real footrace, but the herd is far faster, and Grant knows they're not going to make it.

ABOVE "They're flocking this way": Grant (Sam Neill) flees a stampede of *Gallimimus*.

OPPOSITE LEFT Concept sketch by Mark "Crash" McCreery for a sleek and nimble *Gallimimus*.

STAMPEDE!

In Crichton's novel, Grant and the children run into a stampeding *Hadrosaurus* herd, with the "menacing roar" of the *T. rex* heard in the distance. In his first draft, Crichton removed the apex predator but depicts Grant, Lex, and Tim caught up among a "WALL OF DINOSAURS," including a baby *Triceratops* "squeaking like a pig." They escape by climbing a tree. Crichton's revised draft reinstated the *T. rex* but kept Grant and the kids at a safe distance from the herd: "They see the Rex turn and charge a distant herd of *Hadrosaurs*." Scotch Marmo took it further in her draft with the trio getting caught up in the *Hadrosaurus* stampede before watching the *T. rex* take down a young *Hadrosaur*, an act that "intensely frightens Grant, Lex and Timmy."

Koepp also included a stampede in his drafts, although by his final iteration, the duck-billed *Hadrosaurs* had, at Phil Tippett's suggestion, been replaced by the swifter, sleeker *Gallimimus*. The groundbreaking scene was made possible by Eric Armstrong's cutting-edge work at ILM. Given the technology available at the time, the idea that a herd of lifelike dinosaurs could dart across a landscape, interacting with human performers, was simply unimaginable. Armstrong began building the scene a piece at a time, first building a single digital *Gallimimus* skeleton, and then animating its run cycle.

Once Armstrong had established a realistic running motion, he created a herd of skeletal *Gallimimus* and then composited them into a jungle backdrop. Spielberg was astounded by the result. "I looked at it and I couldn't speak after watching it. I just couldn't even catch my breath. I had never seen anything like it. Because even though it was just a skeletal frame of *Gallimimus*, this herd of *Gallimimus* were moving as realistically as if we had taken a camera and filmed them for real," he says. An ambitious final version of the test footage was then completed, featuring a fully skinned herd of *Gallimimus* running through an environment while being chased by a hungry *T. rex*—a sequence that proved pivotal in Spielberg's decision to replace Phil Tippett's Go-Motion dinosaurs with digital effects. "That was sort of the proof of concept," says Armstrong. "That was a film quality shot, so they knew 'Okay, if you can do that you can basically do anything in the movie.'"

They jump over a huge root network. There's a space under it to hide, and Grant stops the Kids, shoves them underneath, then follows them. They cover their heads as the herd THUNDERS over the roots.

Chunks of everything fly everywhere as the herd plows overhead, their clawed feet striking the roots dangerously close to Grant and the Kids.

Finally, they pass. Grant peers up, over the top root. He looks toward the trees, which the herd is now running alongside.

A ROAR comes from somewhere within the trees.

Grant scans the trees, looking for any sign of the T-rex - -

- - and then it bursts out, ahead of the herd, cutting them off, throwing them into disarray, scattering them everywhere.

They all stare as the rex kicks it into overdrive, runs down one of the Gallimimus, and sinks its teeth into its neck.

The T-rex makes the kill in a cloud of dust and debris. Tim and Grant half rise to their feet, staring in wonder.

LEX
I wanna go - - now!

But Grant and Tim are transfixed,
watching the T-rex.

GRANT
Watch how it eats!

LEX
Please!

GRANT
Bet you'll never look at birds the
same way again!

Tim nods in fascination. The T-rex
pauses in the middle of its meal and
ROARS.

LEX
Let's go!

GRANT
Okay. Keep low. Follow me.

She turns and takes off, running as
fast as she can, across the open
plain. Tim and Grant tear themselves
away and follow her.

TIM
Look at all its blood!

THESE PAGES Storyboards
depict an early version of
the stampede, as the *T. rex*
savages a fleeing *Hadrosaur*.

CUT TO:

INT BUNKER - DAY
ELLIE paces impatiently. She comes down the stairs.

> ELLIE
> Something's happened. Something went wrong.

MULDOON paces too. HAMMOND and MALCOLM are also crammed in the underground bunker. Malcolm lays on a table, while Hammond tries to tend to his wounds.

Hammond speaks, still feeling the obligation of the host.

> HAMMOND
> This is just a delay, that's all this is. All major theme parks have had delays. When they opened Disneyland in 1956, nothing worked, nothing.

> ELLIE
> John . . .

> MALCOLM
> But, John. But if the Pirates of the Caribbean breaks down, the pirates don't eat the tourists.

Another pause. More pacing.

> ELLIE
> I can't wait anymore. Something went wrong. I'm going to go get the power back on.

> MULDOON
> You can't just stroll down the road, you know.

> HAMMOND
> Bob, let's not be too hasty. He's only been gone - - (he looks at his watch)

Muldoon walks over to a steel cabinet. Ellie joins him.

> MULDOON
> I'm going with you.

> ELLIE
> Okay.

Muldoon CLANGS open a steel cabinet, revealing an impressive array of weaponry inside. He removes a shotgun and what looks like a small rocket launcher. He shoves a shell into the barrel of the rocket launcher, which accepts it with a faint electronic SIZZLE.

Hammond searches out the set of blueprints, gets them out of the file cabinet, and spreads them out on top of Malcolm, almost crushing his leg.

> HAMMOND
> Sorry.

Ellie and Muldoon join Hammond.

> HAMMOND (cont'd)
> This isn't like switching on the kitchen light, but I think I can follow this and talk you through it.

Hammond signals with a look.

> ELLIE
> Talk.

> (or)

> Right.

> (nothing)

Ellie gets a couple of walkie-talkies from the shelf and shoves them in her belt.

OPPOSITE Dr. Ellie Sattler (Laura Dern) takes it upon herself to switch the park's power back on.

BACK IN BUSINESS

In the novel, Arnold is killed by a raptor as he tries to switch the power back on in the park's maintenance shed, with the creature standing on his chest before it mauls him to death. Crichton's first script draft sees Arnold caught outside the same building. "The raptors are scrambling over the fence," writes Crichton, "shrieking like hyenas on a blood scent and we know he doesn't stand a chance." In both the novel and the first draft, Gennaro then tries to complete the task but is attacked by a raptor and has to hide from the dinosaur, leaving Grant to finally throw the switch. Crichton's revised draft, however, sees Arnold killed by the raptor, while Gennaro's attempt to turn on the power is dropped; once again it is Grant who switches it back on. In Scotch Marmo's version, it's Sattler who undertakes the hazardous task, accompanied by Muldoon. She also introduced the idea that Sattler is attacked in the maintenance shed by a lunging raptor, which jumps at her from a water pipe. Sattler's bravery remained across Koepp's revisions.

Laura Dern was thrilled with the scenes, particularly as women-led action scenes were still rare at the time. "Other than that, we had not had a lot of experiences of anything but a damsel in distress," she says. Koepp felt it was a natural progression for the character: "It seemed about right for me. Because wallflower characters are no fun to write. So, every character should be active and involved, unless their passivity is the point of the character. Laura's line 'We can discuss sexism in survival situations when I get back'—that's mine. And I think that informed a certain attitude that we wanted to adopt for the film and for her character."

                    ELLIE (cont'd)
                         Okay.

                      HAMMOND
          But you know, I should really be the
                  one going (to go).

                       ELLIE
                         Why?

                      HAMMOND
          Well, because you're a - - I'm a - -

                       ELLIE
                        Look.

                      MULDOON
             Come on, let's go.

OPPOSITE TOP A storyboard panel shows Grant and the kids arriving at the imposing fence that they must scale to get back to the Visitor Center.

                       ELLIE
          We'll discuss sexism in survival
             situations when I get back.

          (she backs towards the door)

          You just take me through this step
             by step. I'm on channel two.

CUT TO:

EXT JUNGLE - DAY

GRANT, TIM, and LEX scramble through the jungle, completely out of breath, exhausted. They arrive at the base of the big electrical fence that surrounds the main compound.

Grant looks up at the fence. It must be over twenty feet high.

                      GRANT
          It's a bit of a climb. You guys
             think you can make it?

                       TIM
                        Nope.

                       Lex
                  Way too high.

Grant grabs a stick and climbs up on the ledge. He looks at the warning light on the fence. It's out. He pokes the wire with a stick. No sparks fly.

                      GRANT
          Well, I guess that means the power's
                        off.

Still not trusting the fence, he taps it with his foot. He moves in slowly and lays both hands on a cable and closes his fingers around it.

Grant's body shakes! He SCREAMS. The kids SCREAM! He stops, and turns around slowly . . . and smiles wickedly.

LEX
That's not funny.

TIM
That was great!

Far in the distance, the T-rex ROARS.
Without a second's delay, both kids
leap to their feet.

CUT TO:

EXT BUNKER - DAY
ELLIE and MULDOON step out of the
bunker.

The main compound feels different
now - - it belongs more to the
jungle than to civilization. Muldoon
has the big gun in his hands.

FLOCKING TO THE AVIARY

Grant's journey with Lex and Tim through the park diverges drastically from Crichton's book. In the novel, they enter an aviary, where they're attacked by *Cearadactylus*. Returning to the raft, they are almost set upon by a group of *Dilophosaurs*, before the *T. rex* arrives. The predator continues its pursuit, the trio finding refuge behind a waterfall. Using its tongue, the *T. rex* tries to drag Tim out of the recess. While Crichton's first draft kept the waterfall sequence, it was absent from all subsequent drafts. Although these scenes didn't make it into the first film, they became showstopper moments in the *Jurassic Park* sequels. The horror of the waterfall attack was saved for *The Lost World*, in which an unfortunate dinosaur trapper meets a watery end. "Steven always liked the idea of the *T. rex* and the waterfall," says Rick Carter. Meanwhile, the aviary became a key set piece in the *Jurassic Park III* finale, with Alan Grant, once again played by Sam Neill, coming up against a flock of *Pteranodons*.

ELLIE
(on the radio)

Okay, I'm on channel two.

MULDOON
Stick to my heels.

They start down the path, moving
quickly.

EXT PATH - DAY
MULDOON and ELLIE emerge from one
path and come into a slightly more
open area. The huge raptor pen stands
silently, surrounded and penetrated
by jungle, the abandoned goon tower
looming over it like a haunted house.

Muldoon slows down, Ellie right next
to him. They notice a hole in the
fence that surrounds the raptor pen.

The metal is twisted, as if gnawed,
the hole is large enough for an
animal to slip through.

ELLIE
Oh my God. Aw, God.

MULDOON
The shutdown must have turned off
all the fences. Goddamn it! Even
Nedry knew better than to mess with
the raptor fence.

He squats near the hole, looking at
the ground. He sees three sets of
footprints. He follows them with his
eyes. They head off in different
directions, but all in the jungle
foliage on either side of them.

MULDOON
C'mon, this way.

ELLIE
I can see the shed from here! We can
make it if we run!

Muldoon walks slowly, as if he heard
something.

ABOVE Sattler (Laura Dern)
and an armed Muldoon
(Bob Peck) leave the bunker
on a mission to reach the
maintenance shed and turn
on the park's power.

OPPOSITE Three
storyboards show an early
incarnation of the scene
in which Sattler leaves for
the maintenance shed.

GAZ-ELLIE

Koepp introduced Sattler in his first draft as "athletic-looking," though he wasn't the first to hit on the idea. As the paleobotanist makes a dash for the shed, Scotch Marmo writes: "Ellie races like a gazelle across the open lawn. She's very fast and graceful." As the writer explains, it was a good character note. "[That] Ellie runs like a gazelle is useful—it is her athleticism that gives her the confidence to switch on the power." This ties in to Marmo's initial Sattler introduction in the early stages of her script: "late 20's, sharp-eyed, tough if she wants to be, runs like a gazelle across the arid land." It was also in stark contrast to her description of Grant: "Good-looking, late 30's, with a thick beard." As she explains, depicting the male lead in that way was deliberate: "I was making fun of all the screenplays I ever read that introduced every single young female as 'good-looking.'"

ABOVE Sattler runs for her life in this storyboard panel.

OPPOSITE A series of storyboards show a planned sequence from earlier drafts where raptors attack the lodge, with one entering through a skylight.

              MULDOON
          No. We can't.

               ELLIE
            Why not?

              MULDOON
    Because we're being hunted. From
        the bushes straight ahead.

Ellie turns, very slowly, to face the bushes. At first, she doesn't see anything, but then there's something very faint, like a shifting of the light, and a shadow seems to move in the bush, RUSTLING the leaves.

              MULDOON
          It's all right.

               ELLIE
          Like hell it is!

Muldoon raises his weapon slowly to his shoulder.

              MULDOON
    Run, towards the shed. I've got her.

Ellie backs up, down the path, slowly. Muldoon follows behind her, keeping his gun trained in the bushes. The shadow in the bushes moves too, at an even pace with them.

              MULDOON
              Go!

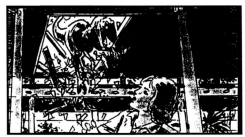

LODGE ATTACK

Crichton's novel features a scene in which Harding, Muldoon, Sattler, Wu, and Malcolm watch as two raptors ferociously gnaw through the bars on the skylight of a room within the park's Safari Lodge. With three other raptors outside in the grounds, Sattler goes out to distract the creatures, allowing Grant—who has safely made it back with the kids—a route to the maintenance shed, where he switches on the power and finds Gennaro in hiding. The two raptors then disappear from the roof, prompting Wu to go outside to warn Sattler—only for the scientist to be savaged to death by a raptor in waiting.

Crichton carried over this set piece into his screenplay drafts, simplifying the outcome slightly: As Sattler returns from distracting the raptors, the door to the lodge is momentarily left open, and Wu is yanked out by the raptor. The sequence never made it past Crichton's drafts, although Scotch Marmo devised a striking death for Wu. Pursued by a raptor, Wu tries to enter Hammond's Quarters where the survivors have gathered, but Muldoon is forced to lock him out to save the others. "I couldn't compromise everyone's safety," he reasons, as Wu's "horrific" screams are heard outside.

Ellie, startled, turns and falls over a log. She quickly stands and starts to run towards the shed. Muldoon walks slowly into the bushes.

ON THE PATH,
Ellie runs as fast as she possibly can - - a real broken field sprint, hopping over branches, flying across the open area at top speed. Over a log - - SPLASH!, she hits a water puddle. She comes to another log obstacle - - she grabs a tree and swings over it.

She nears the maintenance shed, and doesn't look back. She reaches the door, blasts through it, and SLAMS it behind her.

CUT TO:

EXT JUNGLE - DAY
A hand comes into the foreground and takes a firm grip on one of the tight fence cables. Another hand follows it, then a third.

GRANT, TIM, and LEX climb over the fence, pulling themselves up by the tension wires, crawling right past a "DANGER!" sign that tells them this fence ought to be electrified.

INT BUNKER - DAY
MALCOLM and HAMMOND hover over a complex diagram of the maintenance shed that's spread out in front of them. Hammond clutches the radio in his hand, almost praying to it.

Finally, it CRACKLES.

            ELLIE (o.s.)
    I'm in. Mr. Arnold? Mr. Arnold?

INT MAINTENANCE SHED - DAY
ELLIE is at the doorway of the maintenance shed, breathing hard from fear, listening to Hammond's VOICE on the radio.

            HAMMOND (o.s.)
    Great. Good. Okay - - ahead of you should be a metal stairway. Go down it.

Ellie does, heading into the room, shining the flashlight ahead of her. There is a maze of pipes, ducts, and electrical work on both sides of her.

INT SHED - DAY
ELLIE walks straight ahead from the bottom of the metal stairs.

> HAMMOND (o.s.)
> Right. After twenty or thirty feet, you'll come to a T junction. Take a left.

> MALCOLM (o.s.)
> John, just have her follow the main cable - -

> HAMMOND (o.s.)
> I understand how to read a schematic.

Ellie keeps walking, nervous as hell. She looks around. Awfully dark down here.

> ELLIE
> Going down the stairs . . . okay . . . damn it! Dead end!

> HAMMOND (o.s.)
> Wait a minute, wait a minute, there was a right back there somewhere - -

> MALCOLM (o.s.)
> (taking over)
>
> Ellie?! Look above you - - there should be a large bundle of cable and pipes all leading in the same direction! Follow that!

Ellie looks up, finds the bunch of cables, and follows it into a main corridor.

> ELLIE
> (into the radio)
>
> Piping . . . okay . . . following the piping. It goes back up the stairs and across the stairs . . . following the stairs.

> HAMMOND (o.s.)
> Look for a metal grate.

(*ADDED DIALOGUE, NOT RECORDED)

ABOVE Dr. Ellie Sattler navigates Jurassic Park's power grid.

OPPOSITE Two storyboards show Sattler picking her way through the gloomy shed to find the power switch.

ELLIE
Mr. Arnold? He's not answering me.
Okay I'm on the grating.

HAMMOND
Good! Keep going, now. The cable
will terminate in a big, gray box.

ELLIE
Okay, I'm following the tubing. I'm
going down a passage way. How long
does this stuff go for? Could you
guys talk a little bit to me?

(NOTE: DIALOGUE TO BE ADDED,
WASN'T RECORDED - - Steven
Spielberg wants Malcolm to say
something funny to Ellie over the
radio; she smiles)

Walking fast Ellie follows the
tubing to the end of the corridor,
where she sees just a box.

ELLIE
(into the radio)

Okay - - I see the gray box.

Ellie goes through a mesh gate and
walks towards the gray box.

ELLIE (cont'd)
It says "High Voltage."

She pushes the door open even further,
revealing a vast array of breakers and
switches inside.

HAMMOND (o.s.)
Now, Ellie, you can't just throw the
main switch by hand, you have to pump
up the primer handle to give you a
charge. It's a large, flat, gray - -

ELLIE
I see it!

EXT JUNGLE - DAY
GRANT and the KIDS swing over the
top of the fence and start their
climb down.

INT SHED - DAY
ELLIE pumps the gray handle, which
is sluggish. Above it, a small
white indicator CHINGS over from

ABOVE High voltage: Dr.
Ellie Sattler (Laura Dern)
switches the power back on.

OPPOSITE PAGE Storyboard
panels depict tension-building
close-ups as Sattler flicks on
the park's power switches.

"discharged" to "charged." Ellie SLAMS the gray lever back into position.

> ELLIE
> It's charged, okay!

> HAMMOND (o.s.)
> Right (good)! Now, under the words "contact position" there's a round green button that says "push to close!" Push it!

Ellie does. The "contact position" light CHINGS over to "closed" and lights start to go on all over the panel.

> ELLIE
> Did I do it? Is the power back on?

EXT JUNGLE - DAY
GRANT and LEX continue to climb down the fence. Tim is having difficulty - - just as he's about to take another step, he loses his footing and almost falls . . . but then regains control and hangs on.

INT SHED - DAY
ELLIE watches as the column of twelve white indicator lights flash on the control panel. They are clearly labeled, each one for a different area of the park.

> HAMMOND (o.s.)
> Now Ellie, the red buttons turn on the individual park systems. Switch them on.

As Ellie punches the buttons, they light up . . . and our eyes go to near the end of the row.

It's marked "Perimeter Fence."

EXT JUNGLE - DAY
GRANT lets go, dropping the last few feet to the ground. LEX does the same.

A warning light begins to flash, coming back to life. Grant's eyes go wide. He looks up at TIM, who is still far up - - near the top, in fact, he has to come to a complete stop.

ABOVE A terrified Tim (Joseph Mazzello) makes his way over the enormous perimeter fence.

OPPOSITE Storyboards show Tim, Grant, and Lex scaling the fence together.

"YOU'RE CRAZY! I'M NOT GONNA JUMP!"

—TIM MURPHY

INT SHED - DAY
ELLIE keeps pushing the buttons.
She's getting closer to the button
for the fence.

EXT JUNGLE - DAY
TIM, terrified, has frozen where he
is.

                    GRANT
        Tim - - you have to let go!

INT SHED - DAY
ELLIE's still punching the buttons,
now only a half a dozen away from
the one for the fence, now five, now
three - -

EXT JUNGLE - DAY
GRANT and LEX are both screaming at
TIM.

                    GRANT
        C'mon Tim, move down, damn it!

                    LEX
        Timmy! The power is coming back,
                    quick!

                    TIM
        I can't! I'm scared!

                    GRANT
        Tim, you're gonna have to let go.
        I'm going to count to three.

                    LEX
        Jump, Timmy! It's too late!

                    TIM
        I'm afraid I am gonna fall!

GRANT

Go, go, go, jump!

TIM

You're crazy! I'm not gonna jump!

GRANT

Tim, you're going to have to let go of the fence. Tim! Get down right now. Get off the fence! Now!

LEX

Do as he says! The power's coming back, Timmy!

GRANT

Timmy, let go! You're gonna have to let go! Count to three. I'll catch you.

LEX

Timmy! Do as he says! Timmy! Do as Dr. Grant says, quick!

TIM

Are you crazy? What if you miss? I hate it up here.

GRANT

Tim, I'm right here. Easy catch. Easy catch. Count to three.

LEX

You're gonna get electrocuted

(or)

electrified! The power's coming back!

TIM

Shut up! You're scaring me. Stop! You're scaring me.

GRANT

Shhhh. Tim, I'm right here below you. Easy catch. One, two, three. You count it yourself. One, two, three - -

LEX

You're gonna get electrocuted

ON THE FENCE

The idea of Grant and the kids climbing the park's fence on their journey back to the Visitor Center grew in significance as the screenplay evolved. Crichton's iterations had no such idea, but the Scotch Marmo draft sees a nervy Tim climb a twelve-foot-high electrified fence; he loses his footing but makes it over without injury. It wasn't until Koepp's first draft that the fence scene became a more major set piece. "David took it further and Timmy was almost electrocuted. Very nice use of the fence," says Scotch Marmo, admiringly. Koepp intercut the scene with Sattler switching the power back on in the maintenance shed, increasing the tension as Grant urges Tim to jump from the fence seconds before it becomes electrified with 10,000 volts.

(or)

electrified!

GRANT

It's an easy catch, you let - - go - - you do the counting, you count it, Tim. One, two, three - - you do all the counting, okay?

LEX

Timmy, listen to Dr. Grant!

GRANT

I'm coming up there Tim! I'm coming to get you! Lex, I've got to get him!

INT MAINTENANCE SHED - DAY
ELLIE finally pushes the button for
the fences. It stops flashing and
lights up, a brilliant white.

EXT JUNGLE - DAY
The fence HUMS as it awakens. GRANT
and LEX are SCREAMING at TIM:

> TIM
> Okay, okay! I'm going to count to
> three. One, two, three . . .

With a low, loud frightening BUZZ - -

- - the fence comes alive.

POW! Tim is cut off mid-sentence,
and literally thrown from the fence.
He SLAMS into Grant. They fall to
the ground. Lex runs over to them.

> GRANT
> Tim, you're okay? You're okay?

Grant notices a larger problem.

> GRANT (cont'd)
> He's not breathing. Tim?

INT MAINTENANCE SHED
ELLIE watches as the banks of
fluorescent lights in the maintenance
shed come on, one by one.

The lights are going on in rows,
coming closer and closer to her.
Finally, her row comes on. She
follows the light and sees - -

- - a raptor, right there, behind
the control panel! It SLASHES,
taking a lunging sweep at Ellie,
but gets stuck, its feet and legs
tangled in the maze of pipes on the
floor.

This is our first good look at one of
these things, and if it weren't so
terrifying, we could admit that it
truly is a thing of beauty. It's the
biggest of the raptors, intensely
muscled, coordinated as hell, a
smoothly designed predator.

LEFT Sattler (Laura
Dern) attempts to flee the
maintenance shed after
being ambushed by the
raptor that killed Arnold.

OPPOSITE The raptor
crashes into a wire gate in
the maintenance shed.

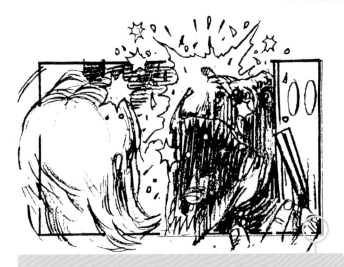

ARMS AND THE MAN

In Koepp's final draft, shortly after Sattler avoids a raptor lunging at her inside the maintenance shed, she backs into a wall, where she discovers what's happened to Ray Arnold. "A dead arm falls onto her shoulder. RAY ARNOLD is there, or what's left of him, stuck in the tangle of pipes," Koepp writes. "She drags the flashlight with her, running over the dead arm and Arnold's legs." In the finished film, only the severed arm is seen. In actual fact, a prosthetic leg was created for the sequence, but Spielberg decided to only use the arm. "I did script his leg," says Koepp. "I think Steven preferred an arm because it could fall over her shoulder." Although Arnold's death in the original book was far more graphic, Koepp says that he never considered showing the character get attacked by a raptor: "No, I didn't write [a death scene]. It was [always] he goes and doesn't come back. And we wonder what's up and then the arm . . . it's very startling."

Ellie SHOUTS and falls back into the pipes on the other side of the aisle.

The raptor untangles itself from the pipes and gives chase, just as Ellie SLAMS the mesh door closed. The raptor BANGS against the mesh door, Ellie falls to the ground.

She holds on by kicking the door shut as the raptor continues to push himself through the door. Ellie is able to get the door closed. She stands, but then falls back onto one of the walls.

A dead arm falls onto her shoulder. RAY ARNOLD is there, or what's left of him, stuck in the tangle of pipes. Ellie moves away, and his arm falls to the ground.

She doesn't realize that she has moved right back near the mesh wall - - and the raptor comes at her again. Ellie takes off running as fast as she can, back the way she came. She drags the flashlight with her, running over the dead arm and Arnold's legs.

She continues to run, her headset dangling, the flashlight dragging behind her on its cord.

She reaches the stairs and hits them hard, flying up them. The raptor must be right behind her, she can hear the CLICKING and CLANGING as it scrambles up the stairs, but she doesn't look back.

She reaches the top, throws open the door, hurls herself outside - -

EXT SHED - DAY
- - and SLAMS the door behind her, just as the raptor's head SNARLS at her from near the top of the stairs. She runs out the fence and collapses.

EXT JUNGLE - DAY
TIM is still unmoving. GRANT is performing CPR, alternately compressing Timmy's chest fifteen times, quickly, and breathing into his mouth twice.

LEX is freaking out.

Fifteen compressions. Two deep breaths.

> GRANT
> C'mon, Tim.

Fifteen compressions. Two deep breaths.

> GRANT
> TIMMY!

Fifteen compress - -

Tim GASPS and comes to.

> GRANT (cont'd)
> Good boy, Tim. Good boy.

> TIM
> Three. (Two, three).

THESE PAGES
Storyboards depict Sattler's raptor encounter in the maintenance shed.

CUT TO:

EXT JUNGLE - DAY
ROBERT MULDOON creeps slowly through
the jungle foliage, tracking his
prey. He ducks and walks through
a hollow log, underneath a fallen
tree, following the RUSTLING sound
up ahead of him.

He can see just a trace of the
raptor's gray flesh as it moves
behind the bushes up ahead, staying
camouflaged enough to deny him a
decent shot. Thinking he's got a
moment, Muldoon extends the back
handle of the gun and clicks it into
place. He prepares to take aim.

A snake slithers across a tree
branch, past what looks like the
large iris of a flower.

The flower blinks.

It's the eye of the raptor. Muldoon
sees it. He raises his gun.

RAPTOR TRAP

The Muldoon death scene gives *Jurassic Park* one of its finest
one-liners, the gamekeeper uttering the phrase "clever girl" as
he realizes he's been flanked by a *Velociraptor*. However, Muldoon's
grisly fate wasn't always sealed. In the novel and drafts by Carter,
Crichton, and Scotch Marmo, Muldoon survives. In the Scotch Marmo
script, he also gets more action scenes, even firing a rocket launcher
at a *Velociraptor*. Koepp's first draft adjusted his fate. Journeying to
the maintenance shed with Ray Arnold, as they embark on a mission
to switch the park's power back on, Muldoon is caught in a pincer
movement by two raptors. About to pull the trigger on one of the raptors,
he mutters "Gotcha" just before the other dinosaur attacks him. That
snippet was eventually dropped in favor of the more poetic "clever girl."

Instead of running away again, the
raptor rises slowly out of the
brush, fully revealing itself to
Muldoon, HISSING at him.

The corners of Muldoon's mouth
twitch up into a smile. He draws a
bead on the animal.

ABOVE The hunter or the
hunted?: Robert Muldoon (Bob
Peck) goes looking for raptors.

OPPOSITE "Clever girl":
One of the raptors that
will seal Muldoon's fate.

His finger tenses on the trigger. Suddenly, his smile vanishes, both eyes pop open, and a terrible thought sweeps across his face. His eyes flick to the side - -

> MULDOON
> Clever girl.

- - which is where the attack comes from. With a ROAR, another raptor comes flashing out of nowhere and pounces on him. The gun BLASTS, but wildly, and the raptor's claw SLASHES through Muldoon's midsection.

Muldoon SCREAMS and falls back, the raptor locked on top of him, all tooth and claw all of a sudden.

As the second raptor makes the kill, the first raptor strides slowly forward and watches approvingly.

It throws its head back and SNARLS.

INT VISITOR'S CENTER - DAY
GRANT, TIM, and LEX come into the deserted visitor's center. A large sign that says "When Dinosaurs Ruled the Earth . . ." droops overhead. Grant now carries Tim, who is weakened but conscious.

> GRANT
> HELLO?!

But nobody answers.

INT RESTAURANT - DAY
GRANT, TIM, and LEX come into the restaurant. Grant carefully sets Tim in a chair at one of the tables. Lex across from him.

> GRANT
> I am gonna have to find the others and get you to a doctor. Will you look after Tim, Lex?

PALEO ART

The "translucent mural" mentioned in Koepp's final draft plays a crucial part in the film. Dividing the Visitor Center restaurant and the lobby, and visible from both rooms, this resplendent frieze, writes Koepp, "depicts dinosaurs in various natural settings," including a *Velociraptor* "in a hunting pose." As the raptors infiltrate the building, the frieze provides the perfect cover for one of the creatures as it stalks Tim and Lex. The actual mural featured in the film consisted of a main panel that was fifteen feet wide and eight feet tall. The mural depicts a raptor and several *Parasaurolophus*, with two side panels that showcase a duo of *Brachiosaurs* and a *Gallimimus*. These dinosaurs were painted by Doug Henderson, a renowned paleoartist and former employee of Phil Tippett, who got the job after Tippett recommended him.

> LEX
> (scared as hell)
> Yes.

Grant nods. He looks at Tim for a second.

> GRANT
> Your hair's all standing up.

He gently rearranges Tim's hair, which is wild, all over his

ABOVE A frazzled-looking Tim (Joseph Mazzello) in the Visitor Center restaurant. Doug Henderson's mural is visible in the background.

OPPOSITE Storyboards depict Muldoon's demise at the claws of a raptor.

FOOD FOR THOUGHT

In Crichton's novel, Lex frequently complains about being hungry when she's out in the park. Koepp decided to drop this idea from his characterization of the girl. "We're all hungry. But we don't want to waste screen time on that," he reasons. However, when the kids reach the Visitor Center, he did make concessions to Lex's hunger pains, writing a scene in which the kids dig into an "all-you-can-eat" buffet. Although it's not specified in Koepp's draft, Tim goes straight for the desserts, while Lex piles some green Jell-O on her plate. "They're starving and they take all the wrong foods! None of them has any nutritional value!" says Koepp.

head. Tim looks up at him weakly and manages a smile. Grant smiles back.

> **GRANT (cont'd)**
> Big Tim, the human piece of toast.

Tim laughs. Grant pauses for a second, as if debating something - -

> **GRANT (cont'd)**
> Be back soon, guys. I promise.

He leaves. As he goes across the lobby of the visitor's center and outside, they can see his silhouette, moving through a translucent mural that depicts dinosaurs in various natural settings. It's quiet for a second as Lex and Tim just look at each other.

Tim goes across the room, to an all-you-can-eat table on the other side, and quickly piles some food on a tray. He brings it back to the table.

Lex digs in, munching on veggies, grabbing food with two hands. Tim enjoys his food, too.

Lex comes up with a spoonful of lime Jell-O from a plastic dinosaur egg cup - - but her hand freezes halfway to her mouth.

Tim looks up, and sees the expression on her face. She's staring over his shoulder, eyes wide, the Jell-O quivering in her shaking hands.

                    TIM
              What?

Tim turns around. Behind him, one of the silhouettes on the mural is a raptor, in a hunting pose.

While they stare, the silhouette of a real raptor moves out from behind it and creeps forward, in the lobby of the visitor's center.

INT KITCHEN - DAY
LEX pulls the shiny metal door shut as quietly as she can. It latches with a distinctive CLICK, but there's no lock.

She runs to a panel of light switches and kills them all, plunging the room into semidarkness. She helps TIM down an aisle and they hide at the end, behind a counter, breathing hard.

GIFTS FOR THE RAPTORS

The Scotch Marmo draft contains a unique moment in which Tim and Lex use windup toys from the Visitor Center gift shop to distract an invading raptor. Inspired by real-life playthings she saw in New York City's Natural History Museum, the writer liked the idea from a metaphorical point of view. "Kids who were almost eaten by a dinosaur can still find the innocence to play with them as toys. It is sort of the definition of some sorts of play—let's make these dangerous beasts into toy size beasts that you have power over instead of the other way around. Plus, the visual of little benign dinosaurs scampering across the floor with a real *T. rex* [in the park] loose is fantastic contrasting imagery."

LEFT Concept art by John Bell shows the gift shop in the Visitor Center, including a Spitter-design umbrella.

OPPOSITE LEFT A storyboard panel shows two raptors making their way through the Visitor Center restaurant.

OPPOSITE TOP After his adventures in Jurassic Park, Tim (Joseph Mazzello) finds every child's dream—an unguarded food buffet.

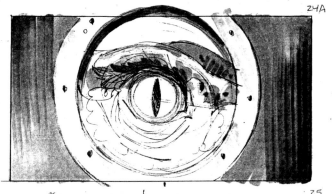

A raptor's head pops into view, visible through the round window in the middle of the restaurant door.

It just looks for a moment, its breath steaming up the window.

ABOVE Storyboards convey the terrifying moment when a raptor uses its claw to open the kitchen door.

OPPOSITE TOP Grant (Sam Neill) and Sattler (Laura Dern) following her escape from the maintenance shed.

THROUGH THE WINDOW,

as the steam evaporates, the raptor can see a part of Tim that is not

entirely hidden by the counter.

IN THE KITCHEN,
TIM and LEX remain frozen in fear as the raptor first SNIFFS at the bottom of the door, then THUMPS its head against it.

But the door doesn't budge.

CUT TO:

EXT COMPOUND DAY
GRANT walks quickly down the narrow path towards Hammond's compound, eyes darting from side to side, not exactly sure where he's going. From far off, he hears someone SHOUTING to him.

He turns. He sees ELLIE, standing outside the bunker. She's waving to him, SHOUTING something too faint for him to hear.

He furrows his brow and walks towards her. She SHOUTS louder. He walks faster. He's closer now, and he can finally make out what she's shouting.

> **ELLIE**
> Run!

Grant takes off running towards her, not even looking back. He races up, and she runs into his arms.

> **ELLIE (cont'd)**
> Where are the kids?!

INT BUNKER - DAY
JOHN HAMMOND stands between GRANT and ELLIE in the bunker, watching as Grant RACKS the bolts on a ten gauge shotgun.

> **GRANT**
> (to Ellie)
>
> It's just the two raptors, right? You're sure the third one's contained?

ELLIE
Yes, unless they figured out how to
open doors.

CUT TO:

INT KITCHEN - DAY

OUTSIDE THE DOOR TO THE KITCHEN,
the raptor stares down at the door
handle, cocking its head curiously.
It SNARLS and bumps the door handle
with its head, but that doesn't do
anything.

It reaches out, toward the handle,
with one clawed hand.

IN THE KITCHEN,
Tim and Lex stare in shock as the
door handle starts to turn.

The door opens. The first raptor
stands in the doorway, draws itself
up to its full height, and looks
around the kitchen.

Now, a second raptor joins it in the
doorway. They move into the room,
brushing against each other. The
first raptor SNAPS at the second, as
if to say "keep your distance."

Now the raptors split, taking two different aisles. Tim and Lex crawl away, Tim awfully weak now, down a third aisle, around the other side of the counter from the raptors, moving in the opposite direction.

As Tim and Lex pass the raptors, one of the raptor's tails SMACK into some pots and pans, knocking them off the counter. They fall on the kids, who manage to keep quiet.

The kids keep moving as one of the raptors dips down, looking through an open cabinet to inspect the racket.

Tim and Lex reach the end of the aisle and round a corner - -

but Timmy's falling behind now, and he accidentally brushes against some hanging kitchen utensils.

Both raptors turn. One jumps onto the counter, knocking more kitchen stuff to the floor. A ladle CLATTERS to a stop, and the strange metallic sounds confuse the raptors for a moment.

But then they move, in Tim's direction, SNIFFING, heading right for him.

The raptor on the floor is just about to turn the corner to where

KITCHEN NIGHTMARES

In the novel's version of the kitchen scene, just one *Velociraptor* is present, which Tim distracts with steaks before locking it in the freezer. The drafts by Crichton and Scotch Marmo stuck to the book, although the latter described the setting as a "huge, industrial kitchen," an upgrade on the novel, which mentions just a stainless steel table, big stove, and walk-in refrigerators. "That really caught Steven's eye, and he went with elaborating that location," she recalls. When building out the scene, Spielberg took inspiration from the Overlook Hotel kitchen seen in Stanley Kubrick's *The Shining* (1980), which features burnished reflective surfaces. The sequence further evolved in Koepp's draft as one raptor became two, and the creatures began displaying problem-solving intelligence. "I think it was Steven who said, 'Can a raptor open a door?'" remarks Rick Carter. "We started thinking 'Well, can a raptor open a door? And would it want to open a door?'" The idea actually has its roots in the novel, in which Crichton describes the raptors' remarkable abilities: "And like chimpanzees, they had agile hands that enabled them to open doors and manipulate objects."

Tim sits, exposed and exhausted, but both the raptors suddenly stop, hearing a CLICKING sound from the other end of the aisle.

It's Lex, TAPPING a spoon on the floor to distract them. The raptor on the counter jumps down and starts cautiously towards Lex's noise, leaving Tim.

Lex sees a steel cabinet behind her, its sliding door slid up and open. She crawls inside, silently.

ABOVE Two storyboards show Tim laying out steaks to lure a raptor into the walk-in freezer, a sequence that came from Crichton's novel but evolved over time.

OPPOSITE On the hunt, a raptor enters the kitchen, where Tim and Lex are hiding.

Tim sees the raptors make the turn towards Lex, SMASHING more stuff around with their tails. He turns and sees a walk-in freezer in the far wall, with a pin-locking handle.

As Lex tries to pull the overhead door to the cabinet shut, one of the raptors rounds a corner and sees her reflection on a shiny cabinet front. Lex tries frantically to lower the cabinet door, but it's stuck.

Tim takes a few deep breaths, summons what little strength he has left - -

- - and makes a break for the walk-in freezer. He's limping, dragging

himself, really moving like a
wounded prey now, and - -

- - the other raptor spots him. Both
raptors go into a pre-attack crouch - -

- - and they pounce, one towards
each of the kids.

Lex tugs on the cover, to no avail - -
Tim's raptor charges after him, just
open floor space between them - -

- - and Lex's raptor THUDS into a
shiny surface bearing her reflection.
It chased the wrong image. It sags
to the floor, semiconscious.

At the other end of the aisle, the
real Lex SCREAMS as the other raptor
bears down on Tim. Tim reaches the
freezer, rips the door open, and
falls inside. The floor is cold and
slick and his feet go right out from
under him. He sprawls across the
floor, rolls out of the way - -

- - and the raptor slips and falls
into the freezer too, right past
him.

Tim drags himself to his feet and
out of the freezer.

The raptor makes one last lunge,
right on Tim's heels, its mouth wide
open - -

- - but Lex SLAMS the door shut
just as Tim is clear. The raptor's
head is caught for a second, but it
SNARLS, retreats, and Lex gets the
door shut all the way.

The raptor ROARS and SCREAMS inside.
Lex jams the pin through the handle,
locking it in.

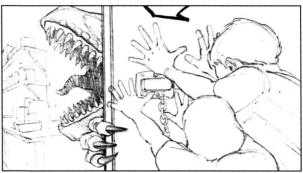

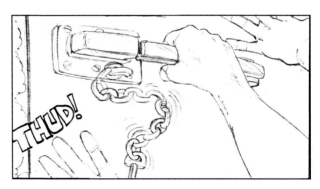

Now the other raptor staggers to its
feet. Groggy, it SMASHES into stuff
all over the kitchen. Lex throws her
arms around Tim again for support
and they take off.

INT RESTAURANT - DAY
TIM and LEX hurry across the
restaurant. They stare back over
their shoulders as they run. They
CRASH into GRANT and ELLIE.

ABOVE Storyboards show
Tim and Lex locking the
raptor in the freezer.

OPPOSITE TOP Tim (Joseph
Mazzello) hides from two
raptors in the kitchen.

OPPOSITE BOTTOM Lex
distracts a raptor by banging
a ladle on the ground in
this storyboard panel.

LEX
It's in there!

ELLIE
Control room.

INT SECOND FLOOR CORRIDOR - DAY
GRANT, ELLIE, and the KIDS race down the second floor corridor towards the control room, Grant helping Tim.

INT CONTROL ROOM - DAY
The door to the control room SMACKS open. GRANT, ELLIE, and the KIDS burst in. Ellie heads straight for Nedry's computer terminal.

Grant moves Tim to the side, and races back to the door to lock it.

LEX
We can call for help?!

ELLIE
We've got to reboot the system first!

She sits at the computer and studies the screen. It's flashing at her, dominated by a maze-like grid. She studies it, confused.

GRANT
(at the door)

Oh, no! The door locks - - Ellie! Boot up the door locks! Boot up the door locks!

POW! Something hits the door, hard, from the outside, the kids SCREAM, Grant hurls his back against it - - Grant loses his gun. He struggles. The raptor scratches his head.

ELLIE
ALAN!

- - and Ellie leaps out of the chair and races over to the door to help him. A raptor SNARLS and

SNAPS, RAMMING itself against the door, trying to force its way into the control room. It's all Ellie and Grant can do to hold the door against the onslaught, but it bucks against them viciously.

> GRANT
> (to Ellie)
>
> Ellie - - get back and boot up the door locks!

> ELLIE
> You can't hold it by yourself!

> GRANT
> Ellie, get the gun!
>
> (or)
>
> Try to reach the gun!

> ELLIE
> I can't get it!
>
> (or)
>
> I can't get it unless I move!

LITTLE SQUIRT

In the storyline created by Rick Carter for his working document, when the children leave the kitchen, after locking one raptor in the freezer, they are confronted by the second raptor back in the restaurant. To prevent an attack, Tim takes an umbrella from the gift counter to use as a makeshift weapon. Pointing it at the creature like a sword, the umbrella opens, revealing an image of a *Dilophosaurus* emblazoned on its outer canopy, a sight that stops the raptor in its tracks. Coincidentally, a similar idea would be utilized in Colin Trevorrow's *Jurassic World* (2015) when a *Dilophosaurus* hologram similarly flummoxes a raptor.

In Carter's document, Tim also presses a button on the umbrella, which squirts water at the raptor. "The idea of an umbrella squirting water is pretty ridiculously funny," says Carter. "You have this thing designed to keep the water out. It's actually squirting water!" The concept of a branded novelty umbrella came up during brainstorming sessions, adds Carter, when he and others on the team began to consider, "How would the dinosaur experience be commercialized in that park, and that Visitor Center?" It's not the only humorous moment that Carter came up with. Before the kitchen scene in Carter's version, the raptors are seen in the restaurant. One sniffs some potato salad which causes it to sneeze. "I think that would be me trying to be like Steven. Personalizing what the response would really be for a dinosaur taking on our world," says Carter. The scene ends with the raptor devouring a cake, its jaws covered in frosting. The second raptor then licks the frosting off its companion's face.

KEYBOARD WARRIORS

In the novel, it's the older version of Tim who navigates the Jurassic Park computer system to help restore power. With the ages of the characters switched around for the film, Koepp made Lex the digital expert. "I can't claim visionary feminist sensibilities in having her be the one who figures out the computer system . . . that's really a function of age," he says. Impressively, when she sits down at the Silicon Graphics workstation, she even recognizes the operating system—Unix. "Always ahead of his time, Mr. Spielberg," remarks Joseph Mazzello. "I do think about that a lot. You would never even dream of having the computer nerd be the girl. That's like the last sort of person back then that you would think to cast in that kind of role, and yet it works absolutely perfectly."

ABOVE Concept art by Ed Verreaux, showing a variation on the raptor smashing through the Control Room window. Here, it's depicted on a glass roof.

OVER AT THE COMPUTER,
Lex slides quickly into the command chair at Nedry's terminal. She stares at the screen for a moment - -

                    LEX
This is a Unix system. I know this.

It's the files for the whole park.
It's like a phone book - - it tells
         you everything.

- - and then her fingers start to
fly over the keyboard. Tim watches,
amazed, as the computer starts to
respond to Lex's commands.

                 LEX (cont'd)
I've got to find the right file. Oh
no, this isn't right. This might be
       right, no this isn't it.

                    TIM
C'mon, Lex! C'mon, Lex! Go, Lexie!

Reaching another menu, Lex spots a
box on the screen that reads "DOOR
INTEGRITY." She reaches out and
touches it. The screen BEEPS - -

                    LEX
There it is, I got it! This is it, I
          did it. Yes, yes!

- - and the door latch panel BUZZES. Grant and Ellie put everything they have into it and finally the door SNICKS shut, locking the raptor outside.

                    GRANT
            What works?

                    LEX
    Phone, security systems, everything
    works. You ask for it, we got it!

CUT TO:

INT BUNKER - DAY
A phone RINGS. HAMMOND and MALCOLM look at each other, wide-eyed. Hammond lunges for it.

                    HAMMOND
        Grant?!· The children alright?

INT CONTROL ROOM - DAY
All the screens in the control room have come alive now, and data is scrolling by at incredible speed as every remaining system in the park comes back on line. ELLIE is at the keyboard with LEX now, figuring things out, and GRANT is on the phone.

                    GRANT
            The children are fine.

INT BUNKER - DAY
HAMMOND is on the phone, MALCOLM is trying to listen.

                    HAMMOND
            Thank God.

                    GRANT (o.s.)
    Listen, the phones are back up! Call
    the mainland! Tell them to send the
            damn helicopters - -

Suddenly Grant stops in the middle of his sentence. A SCREAM cuts in, then three GUNSHOTS, fast, and a horrible CLUNKING as the phone is dropped.

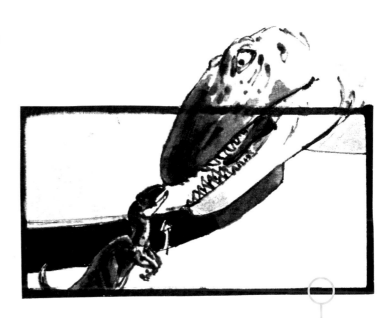

PARENTAL CONTROL

In Crichton's novel, during the raptor attack on the compound, Tim, Lex, and Grant witness the grim fate of a baby raptor, a creature they encountered earlier in the hatchery. Two adult raptors fight over the squealing baby, devouring it between them. Rick Carter's working document takes a different tack, when Grant and the kids are confronted in a dinosaur nursery by a snarling adult raptor. The quick-thinking Lex opens the cage where the baby raptor is housed. It first jumps on her shoulder before heading toward "the first adult raptor it's ever seen." The raptor picks up the baby in its mouth and runs away, protecting the infant creature in a far less gruesome conclusion. "That's exactly where Crichton meets Spielberg. Take a Crichton situation, but you give it a slightly more optimistic outcome," says Carter. Although Carter's idea would not be used, the notion that raptors could be protective, doting parents would be explored in *Jurassic Park III*. Many years later, the idea would be developed even further in *Jurassic World: Dominion* (2022) through the raptor character Blue and the deep bond she shares with her hatchling, Beta.

ABOVE A storyboard panel depicts an adult raptor about to carry a hatchling away to safety.

SHIP OF FOOLS

The last act of Crichton's novel features a ticking time bomb in the form of supply ship the *Anne B* unwittingly carrying live raptors toward the mainland. As it heads toward Puntarenas, it's a race against time to re-establish radio communications. When Tim manages to hail the ship, Gennaro demands that the crew turn around, telling them they'll be in violation of "Section 509 of the Uniform Maritime Act," something he makes up on the spot. The drafts by Crichton and Scotch Marmo give that speech to Grant, as he warns the ship they are carrying "stolen biological materials." When Koepp came on board, the idea of raptors or stolen eggs/embryos leaving the island was permanently dropped from the storyline.

ABOVE DNA sequencing code is projected onto the head of the raptor after it bursts into the Control Room.

OPPOSITE TOP A storyboard panel shows Lex hanging from the air duct as she narrowly avoids the jaws of a raptor beneath her.

HAMMOND
Grant! GRANT! But there's no answer.

INT CONTROL ROOM - DAY
Grant's rifle lies on the floor, smoking, several spent shells alongside it. The front window of the control room has three huge impact shatter patterns in the glass, where the gunshots hit.

TIM goes into an open panel through the ceiling, and into the crawl space. LEX climbs the ladder, followed by ELLIE and GRANT.

Grant looks over to the front window, scared as hell, just as -

-- it SHATTERS in a shower of glass and a raptor EXPLODES into the control room. It lands on its feet on a workstation console, images from wall projectors falling across its head.

Grant vaults himself up into the ceiling, and knocks the ladder with his feet.

The raptor tilts its head curiously, looking up at the swaying ceiling.

IN THE CRAWL SPACE,
Grant, Ellie, and the kids dash across the ceiling panels, moving fast, but carefully, so as not to break through.

SMASH! The raptor's head bursts
through a panel behind them, leaping
up at them, SNARLING and SNAPPING.

It drops down again, and they keep
moving forward. But now it ERUPTS
through a panel right in front of
them. They SCREAM, its teeth CLICK
just inches in front of Ellie - -

- - but the raptor can't hold itself
up there, and it falls back to the
floor of the control room.

Grant looks around frantically and
spots an air duct a few yards away.

                GRANT
            Follow me!

OUT OF CONTROL

In the novel, the raptors who break into the compound don't
make it to the Control Room. It wasn't until Koepp's first draft, in
which one of the creatures smashes its way into the park's nerve
center, that a key part of the film's finale started to take shape.
In the scene, Grant drops the phone he is using to speak to
Hammond. "The raptor bends over it and crushes it in its mouth,"
wrote Koepp, a chilling moment. The screenwriter, however,
crosses out the sentence, as part of his handwritten revisions,
and the moment was absent from any subsequent drafts.

They move for it, but the raptor's
head CRASHES through the ceiling
again, this time right underneath
Lex.

She SCREAMS and is lifted up, on top of its head, and pinned to the ceiling above.

ABOVE Storyboards show a raptor smashing its head through an air duct and receiving a boot in the face from Grant.

Grant SMASHES his boot into the side of the raptor's head. The raptor SNAPS at him, latching onto his boot for a second before the raptor's own weight pulls it back down.

OPPOSITE TOP Early storyboards showing Grant poisoning dinosaur eggs and feeding them to raptors.

Lex goes down with the raptor, spinning into the hole in the ceiling, tumbling down. Grant grabs her by the collar at the last second, but Lex dangles there, above the raptor.

The animal flips over onto its feet and crouches to pounce just as Grant summons his strength and jerks Lex back into the ceiling.

The raptor springs, but too late. Grant and Lex scramble over to the air duct and join Ellie and Tim inside it.

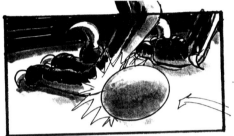

IN THE AIR DUCT,

Grant, Ellie, and the kids crawl through the air duct as fast as they can, the thin metal BOOMING and creasing around them. They reach a metal gate that shows daylight beneath. Grant reaches out and pulls it up.

Through the gate, they can see the lobby of the visitor's center below. They're directly above the skeletons of the dinosaurs, the T-rex and the sauropod it's attacking. The unfinished skeletons are surrounded by scaffolding.

INT ROTUNDA - DAY

GRANT and the OTHERS climb down out of the air duct and onto a platform of the scaffolding that stands alongside the skeletons. They continue down to the second platform, then the third. They suddenly see - -

A raptor, standing to the side by the second floor railing.

It's much too far to jump to the lobby floor, so Grant climbs gingerly

REQUIEM FOR THE RAPTORS

From the novel to the screenplays, the fate of the raptors differs wildly. In the book and Crichton's drafts, Grant kills two raptors by feeding them eggs injected with toxins and injects poison directly into the tail of a third. In Scotch Marmo's draft, the poisoned eggs idea was nixed, and a new form of raptor death was devised. With the kids hiding inside the rib cage of a *T. rex* skeleton as the raptor desperately tries to claw at them, Grant saves the day by grabbing onto a piece of scaffolding and using it to smack the *T. rex* skeleton, shattering the neck and causing the head to fall and crush the raptor to death. Similarly, in Koepp's first draft, the final raptor gets tangled up in the jaws of the *T. rex* skeleton and is killed by Grant who uses a workman's mechanical lift to compress the bones of the model and crush the beast to death.

onto the nearest skeleton, the towering brachiosaur.

They climb down as fast as they can. Grant helps Tim down, Lex and Ellie follow. Ellie goes to the tail. Lex moves to the front.

Grant lands on the main body in the middle with Tim. And the raptor watches them.

Up in the ceiling, the skeleton's anchor bolts GROAN in the plaster, starting to pull free. But for now, they hold.

The raptor flies out and lands on the back of the middle section of the skeleton. SNAP! It CRACKS apart with the weight, sending the sections spinning in all different directions.

Grant and Tim twirl on the middle section. Tim begins to slide down. Grant tries to hold on to him - - but Tim loses his grip and falls to the ground right underneath the swinging, large middle section of the dinosaur skeleton.

Meanwhile, Lex spins on the front section. She slips - - and tries to keep from falling as she hangs by her legs.

The anchor bolts in the ceiling RIP free, ZINGING past them like bullets. The entire brachiosaur skeleton collapses like a house of cards sending Ellie to the ground. She covers herself with her arms, trying to protect her head from the shower of falling bones.

Lex falls, landing on the ground with bones falling on top of her. She SCREAMS.

Grant, alone in the middle section, looks up and sees the cable about to SNAP - - he falls! The large section of the skeleton comes careening down, heading straight for Tim, who lays where he fell on the ground. It comes SMASHING down . . . with just enough space for him to be safe.

The raptor tumbles to the floor in a cascade of splintering bone.

THESE PAGES A series of storyboards depict a sequence in which Grant, Sattler, and the kids descend from the air duct and onto scaffolding platforms in the Visitor Center lobby.

It lands on its back a few yards away and staggers for a moment, the wind knocked out of it.

Grant lands in front of Tim. He stands, and goes to Tim. Lex sits up and sees the raptor regain its feet. She SCREAMS.

Ellie stands. She notices the shadows of the second raptor, standing behind the Visqueen. She stops dead in her tracks. She backs up towards Grant and Tim.

The raptor comes out from under the plastic and looks around.

Grant gets Tim out from under the skeleton. Lex joins them. They back away from the raptor, approaching from the left side. They back up towards the large rock in the middle of the room holding the other skeleton.

GRANT LOWERS TIMMY DOWN...

THESE PAGES Storyboards illustrate the chaos caused by a relentless raptor as it jumps onto a dinosaur skeleton, breaking it and leaving Grant, Sattler, and the kids in free fall.

The raptors crouch in their pre-attack stance - -

The group is caught in the middle of the two approaching raptors.

Lex looks back and SCREAMS. Grant and the others continue to back up. They look up and see - -

- - TYRANNOSAURUS REX! Its massive head descends down from above. A set of six-foot jaws clamp down on the raptor. Eighteen-inch teeth sink into its side, and the helpless animal HOWLS in agony as it's lifted up, up, up off the floor of the lobby.

Grant and the others look up in stunned amazement. They step back behind the rock for safety and look to the right. They see another raptor approaching.

The other raptor goes up in the air now, twenty feet off of the lobby floor, held fast in the mouth of the Rex. It stands in the entrance to the lobby in front of the massive hole it ripped through the Visqueen wall. It shakes its enormous head once, BREAKING the neck of the velociraptor, then drops it, dead, to the floor at its feet.

Grant, Ellie, and the kids skirt the battle royal on the lobby floor and dash out of the door of the Visitor's Center.

The second raptor turns from the humans and lunges at the Rex's side, leaping twelve feet into the air and rending the Rex's flesh as it comes down, slashing it open with its six-inch claw.

REX RETURNS

It was Steven Spielberg who came up with the idea of bringing the *T. rex* back to battle the two raptors, the dinosaur inadvertently saving Grant and the others. The new direction came midway through the shoot, a period when Koepp was working in his office on the Universal lot, close to the soundstages where the film was being shot. "I went down to the set, and [Spielberg] said, 'You know, the ending . . .' I said, 'Yes?' He said, 'It's not that I don't like the ending we have. It's that I love the *T. rex* so much. I've seen enough to know that really works. And it's got to come back.'" It was pure instinct on Spielberg's part, asserts Rick Carter: "He just knew what he wanted. He needed to have that Rex come back and save the day." When Koepp quizzed the logic of the scene, wondering how Grant and the others wouldn't see the *T. rex*'s arrival, Spielberg was unfazed: "Steven said, 'No, they wouldn't, there's raptors over here!' He said, 'The audience is looking at the raptors. And so are the characters. You don't think about that unless I show it.' And he's right. I mean, some people, of course said, 'Why wouldn't we see it?' But I don't think those people would trade the moment for that tiny bit of believability." Brushing aside these logical concerns, it's the perfect ending. "The *T. rex* becomes a hero," says Carter. Or as Koepp puts it, "Instead of the defeat of the park, or the defeat of Hammond, it evolved into the triumph of the animals."

The rex BELLOWS in pain, and turns on the raptor, eyes raging, and strikes, just once, quickly, as fast as the head of a serpent. It catches the raptor by its thick back end, puts one of its enormous feet down on it, and tears.

It rips the last velociraptor in half.

The rex whirls around - as it turns, its heavy tail counterbalances, SNAPPING the other way, sweeping across the lobby, and SMASHING right through the T-rex skeleton.

The skeleton collapses in an explosion of bones, falling to pieces around the living rex.

The rex stands majestically in the middle of the lobby, both skeletons swept away, SNAPPING like matchsticks as they settle around the animal.

The rex draws itself up to its full height - -

- - and ROARS.

ABOVE The *T. rex* saves the day, savaging the two raptors.

OPPOSITE Grant (Sam Neill), Sattler (Laura Dern), Lex (Ariana Richards), and Tim (Joseph Mazzello) watch in amazement as the *T. rex* defeats the raptors.

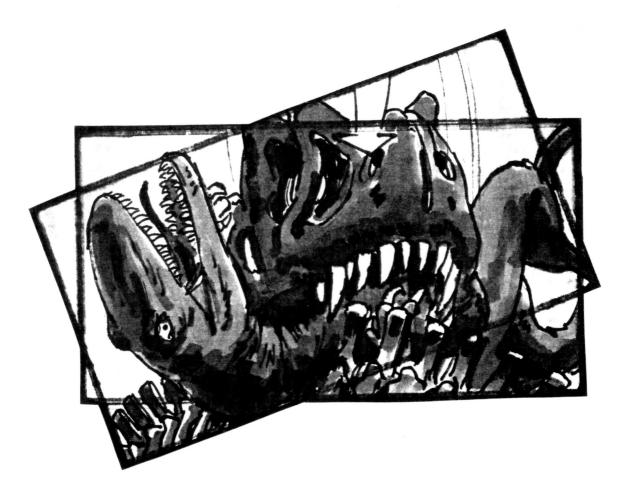

The sound is deafening, and the vibrations rattle the entire Visitor's Center. The sign which dangled over the lobby by its one remaining wire finally falls, CLATTERING to the floor at the Rex's feet, face up.

"WHEN DINOSAURS RULED THE EARTH," it says.

OUTSIDE THE VISITOR'S CENTER
Hammond SQUEALS the Jeep to a halt in front of the steps. Malcolm is lying in the back.

Grant and the others practically fall into the Jeep.

>   GRANT
>   Mr. Hammond, I've decided not to
>   endorse your Park.

BANNER DAY

One of *Jurassic Park*'s most evocative visual moments plays like a curtain call. "The *T. rex* finally took that moment for a bow and roared so memorably," says Koepp. As the dinosaur lets out a triumphant cry, the "When Dinosaurs Ruled the Earth" banner in the Visitor Center flutters to the ground. The shooting script has a slightly different take on the scene: "The sign, which dangled over the lobby by its one remaining wire, finally falls, CLATTERING to the floor at the Rex's feet, face up." Says Koepp, "I wanted it to smack into the ground and rattle to a stop the way those things do. And Steven changed it, of course, to the lovely fluttery banner." A CG shot, the fluttering banner worked perfectly. "His version was, of course, much more lyrical," says Koepp.

ABOVE The *T. rex* lets it be known that dinosaurs still rule the Earth.

OPPOSITE Storyboards from an earlier iteration of the finale, showing a raptor being crushed to death in the jaws of the *T. rex* skeleton.

SURVIVOR'S INSTINCT

In Koepp's drafts, John Hammond survives to witness the impact of his own hubris, but it wasn't always this way. In the novel, Crichton's visionary entrepreneur takes a tumble down a steep hillside and breaks his ankle. Shouting for help, he's gradually surrounded by Compys, as one jumps on his chest and begins chewing his neck. Crichton's first draft riffs on this idea. Hammond is pinned to the floor by a fallen dinosaur bone in the Visitor Center, before a pack of Compys arrives and gets to work. Crichton's revised draft sees an injured Hammond in the park's projection booth; as raptors come for him, his bloodcurdling cries can be heard alongside the sound of the narration he recorded for the tour's informational film.

Rick Carter's working document sees Hammond clawed by a raptor before falling to his death, landing on a scale model of Jurassic Park—a "poetic" denouement, according to the production designer. The Scotch Marmo iteration takes one element from Crichton's novel, depicting him stumbling down a hill, but stops short of savaging him. He's last seen alive, partly submerged in water, as a mosquito lands on his hand. The writer liked the idea of leaving him alone on the island. "I could not imagine that Hammond would leave his island with the others," she says. "It was his monster and he loved it. Why would he abandon it? He was also delusional about the danger."

Although Koepp felt the novel's scheming version of Hammond "had it coming," the casting of Sir Richard Attenborough and the steering of the character toward a more Walt Disney–like figure meant death did not become him. "As the character changed, that fate did not seem appropriate," he says. However, Koepp's first draft did contain a story beat somewhat similar to Carter's moment where Hammond collapses on the model park; when Grant shoots a raptor dead, it falls onto a life-size cardboard cutout of Hammond, ripping through the effigy's head. "There was a sense that you want some sort of symbolism with the final images and to tie into something else that makes you think of the bigger picture," comments Koepp.

HAMMOND
After careful consideration, Dr. Grant - - so have I.

Hammond hits the gas and the Jeep takes off.

EXT HELICOPTER LANDING PAD - DAY
The helicopter rotors whirl to life as the chopper waits on the landing cross. Two Jeeps ROAR up next to it, one driven by GRANT, the other by HAMMOND.

INT HELICOPTER - DAY
One by one, they climb aboard, their faces white from their ordeal.

ELLIE comes on first, holding LEX. Then HAMMOND, carrying TIM. And GRANT, helping MALCOLM.

No one speaks. Hammond takes another look at his dream, Grant comes over and takes him back to the helicopter.

The helicopter takes off immediately. As they rise into the air, they stare out the windows, looking down on the park as it spreads out below.

DOWN IN THE PARK,
the helicopter soars over a vast plain. The Tyrannosaur, which is still feeding on the remains of the dinosaurs it ran down and killed, looks up.

It throws its head back and ROARS, waving its little forelimbs at the strange thing in frustration. As the helicopter moves off, the T-rex just stares, silently, with huge, yellowing eyes. It's a moment of utter bewilderment for the rex, and we almost feel - -

- - sad for her.

DENOUEMENT

The novel sees Isla Nublar blown to smithereens by the Costa Rican military, an idea that Crichton kept for his first draft in which helicopters loaded with "armaments" obliterate the island. In Crichton's revised draft, this violent denouement was dropped in favor of something more benign, as a rescue helicopter collects the survivors and leaves Isla Nublar behind: "Now we have a moment of primordial jungle sounds, nature as it once was, undisturbed." Rick Carter's working document featured a much more dramatic idea that came from Spielberg's fertile mind: As Malcolm, Grant, and the others leave, the *T. rex* bites the skid of the helicopter, sending it spinning out of control. As Grant hoists himself up into the chopper, the dinosaur even manages to rip off one leg of his pants! "The idea of the *T. rex* jumping up and grabbing somehow Grant's pants and ripping them off would be a Spielbergian idea," confirms Carter. Scotch Marmo's draft also featured a similar *T. rex*/helicopter moment, although without the pants-ripping gag. Koepp recalls nothing about this ending: "I was not privy to that one. Steven must have moved on from that before I got there." Instead, Koepp's finale returns to something akin to Crichton's revised draft, as the helicopter lifts the survivors away to safety. The final draft added a scene featuring the *T. rex* in her natural habitat, letting out another mighty roar, although this moment did not make the movie. Koepp concludes his final draft with the helicopter skimming over a flock of seabirds—a potent grace note, and a reminder of the evolutionary connections between dinosaurs and birds.

ABOVE A storyboard panel related to the Carter / Scotch Marmo drafts depicts the *T. rex* biting the skid of the escape helicopter.

OPPOSITE TOP Crichton's second draft sees Hammond killed offscreen by a raptor in a projection booth. Here, in a variation on that theme, he's killed in the theater.

BACK IN THE HELICOPTER,
Hammond looks down at the park, his
eyes full. He looks over at the kids.

They're in the back of the
helicopter, with Grant. As they look
out the window, Grant almost absently
has his arms around both kids.

Now Ellie looks at him. Both he
and the kids seem so natural, so
obviously comfortable and trusting
with each other. She smiles.

The four of them sit that way, in
the back of the helicopter, huddled
together. Survivors.

Grant looks out the window.

The helicopter sweeps low over
a huge flock of sea birds that's
feeding on a school of fish. As the
chopper ROARS near, it kicks up the
flock. Hundreds of birds sail off
in all directions, powerful and
graceful.

Grant looks at the birds and breaks
into a wide grin.

The birds reform as a flock again and
fly straight into the sun.

FADE OUT.

ABOVE The majesty of
Jurassic Park is captured
in this early concept art
by Tom Cranham.

OPPOSITE PAGE Storyboards
show the abandoned sequence
in which the T. rex attacks
the departing helicopter.

INSIGHT
EDITIONS

PO Box 3088
San Rafael, CA 94912
www.insighteditions.com

Find us on Facebook: www.facebook.com/InsightEditions

Follow us on Twitter: @insighteditions

Follow us on Instagram: @insighteditions

All rights reserved. Published by Insight Editions, San Rafael, California, in 2024.

ISBN: 979-8-88663-331-3

Publisher: Raoul Goff
VP, Co-Publisher: Vanessa Lopez
VP, Creative: Chrissy Kwasnik
VP, Manufacturing: Alix Nicholaeff
VP, Group Managing Editor: Vicki Jaeger
Publishing Director: Chris Prince
Art Director: Matt Girard
Editor: Harrison Tunggal
Editorial Assistant: Emma Merwin
Managing Editor: Maria Spano
Senior Production Editor: Katie Rokakis
Senior Production Manager: Joshua Smith
Senior Production Manager, Subsidiary Rights: Lina s Palma-Temena

ROOTS of PEACE   REPLANTED PAPER

Insight Editions, in association with Roots of Peace, will plant two trees for each tree used in the manufacturing of this book. Roots of Peace is an internationally renowned humanitarian organization dedicated to eradicating land mines worldwide and converting war-torn lands into productive farms and wildlife habitats. Roots of Peace will plant two million fruit and nut trees in Afghanistan and provide farmers there with the skills and support necessary for sustainable land use.

Manufactured in China by Insight Editions

10 9 8 7 6 5 4 3

ACKNOWLEDGMENTS

This is my third Jurassic-related project for Insight Editions, and as the film marks its 30th anniversary in 2023, it never ceases to amaze me the passion that people have for this film. So, a huge thank you to everyone who helped make this book what it is.

Firstly, I'd like to thank my editors on this project, Chris Prince and Harrison Tunggal, whose impeccable guidance, ideas, and enthusiasm turned this into a really special project. I would also like to thank all those that helped lay out and design this book, including Matt Girard and Lola Villanueva. Beautiful work.

For their time and wonderful recollections during my research period, I'd like to thank Steven Spielberg and Kathleen Kennedy, without whom I'd be lost on Isla Nublar.

With this being a book devoted to the *Jurassic Park* screenplay, my eternal gratitude goes to screenwriter David Koepp, who generously gave up his time amid his hectic schedule to talk about his work. Likewise, the brilliant Rick Carter, whose knowledge of the Jurassic universe helped elevate this book. I'd also like to thank Malia Scotch Marmo for digging back into her archives and providing some incredible insight.

Huge thanks also to: Ed Verreaux, John Bell, David Lowery, Dennis Muren, Phil Tippett, Michael Lantieri, Randal Dutra, Dean Cundey, Michael Kahn, John Williams, Jack Horner, John Rosengrant, Shane Mahan, Lindsay Macgowan, Alan Scott, Gary Hymes, Gary Rydstrom, Janet Hirshenson, Ariana Richards, Joseph Mazzello, Sam Neill, Jeff Goldblum, Laura Dern, Steve "Spaz" Williams, Stefen Fangmeier, Mark Dippé, Eric Armstrong, Kelly Porter, Mitchell Ray Kenney, Craig Mullins, Tom Cranham, David J. Negron, John Gurche, Mark "Crash" McCreery, Masako Masuda, Paul Sonski, Marty Kline, Jim Teegarden, Caroline Quinn, Mark Hallett, Stefan Dechant, and Dan Sweetman.

I'd also like to extend a special thanks to Astrid Vega and especially to Derrick Davis. Without your contributions, suggestions, and resources, Derrick, this book wouldn't be what it is. Thank you.

And thank you to the folks at Universal who supported the creation of this book.

Finally, I'd like to dedicate this book to Julie, for somehow remaining sane throughout the continued talk about *Jurassic Park* in our household.